WORDS IN OUR TIME

By the same author

IVOR BROWN'S BOOK OF WORDS

I GIVE YOU MY WORD

SAY THE WORD

NO IDLE WORDS

HAVING THE LAST WORD

I BREAK MY WORD

A WORD IN EDGEWAYS

CHOSEN WORDS

IVOR BROWN

WORDS
IN OUR TIME

JONATHAN CAPE
THIRTY BEDFORD SQUARE · LONDON

PRINTED IN GREAT BRITAIN IN THE CITY OF OXFORD
AT THE ALDEN PRESS
BOUND BY A. W. BAIN & CO. LTD, LONDON

FOREWORD

My excuse for making yet another Word Book is both familiar and contemptible. 'Please, sir, he began it.' My friend Norman Edwards, when he was editor of *Everybody's*, asked me to contribute some explanations of terms in common use. He, as well as I, had noticed the verbal paradox of our times; while the section of the community which has been classically educated grows proportionately smaller, the number of classical words introduced by the sciences goes soaring up. Thus many are continually talking Greek, as M. Jourdain talked prose, without knowing it. Now millions of people are using names whose origin they could not begin to explain: and sometimes it is plain that they are vague about the meaning of the terms they fling about. It is said on every side that the British people must have more and more scientific training and bigger and better laboratories, not only to make bigger and better bombs. At the same time the men of science, instead of trying to accommodate their terminology to the common understanding, pile up words of many syllables based on Latin or Greek roots and frequently on a clumsy mixture of both. These monsters are certainly bigger: but they can hardly be deemed better.

In the academies of science a new language has, no doubt, to be found to cope with the newly discovered elements and forces. Since the Greeks began so much of man's inquiry into the nature of things, it is reasonable that the new vocabulary of the sciences should be derived from the ancient world and its word-formations. What is strange and unnecessary is the importation of prolix classical terms into spheres where there is no need for them. The psychologists have created a turgid and pretentious jargon of their own, much as the ordinary doctor continues to impose on the ordinary man by writing his prescriptions in Latin and ending his mysterious communication with the absurd pedantry of adding 'Mitte', instead of 'send' as his command to the chemist. The ordinary man has occasionally exploited this by using the 'psycho' lingo himself and turning it to his own purposes. I was told of a private soldier on charge. Had he any reason or excuse for his drunken violence? 'Yes, sir,' came the reply. 'I suffer from a post-traumatic neurosis.' That sort of affliction was once called by simpler names, such as shell-shock; and preferably so.

The flow of these classical terms into the politics of a democracy where simplicity and lucidity are most desirable is another current nuisance. Why should the common reader who is endeavouring to sum up the results of an election deciding his own fate be confronted with words like Psephology and Demographical? Both are translated in this book, whose purpose has been to explain the sources and meanings of some of the principal alien words with which the citizen is so often confused.

I find it hard to understand why writers are so much fascinated by any new classicism that is foisted on us: journalists appear to think that they can establish themselves as smart, up-to-date fellows if they plaster their articles with these new-comers. For example, at the time of writing, Monolithic has just come into fashion and is being applied loosely to anything single or solid. Monolith is a word of Greek origin used to describe a single stone, especially those single, monumental stones that have been left by the peoples of the late Stone Age about our countryside along with the trilithic (three-stoned) or polylithic (many-stoned) erections of a huge temple such as those of Avebury or Stonehenge. Why the monolith has been dragged into politics, I do not know. But once somebody had written of Russia as a monolithic society, monolithic was accepted because it looked imposing and showed signs of learning. It was almost at once applied to other kinds of solid structure. Monolithic societies do not have genuine elections, so that psephologists are not needed therein, but the 'vital statistics of the demographical expert' certainly are required. It is noteworthy that European Communism has itself favoured an extremely academic and classical vocabulary. It dotes on a Praesidium. If classical scholars sometimes deem themselves the remnant champions of a lost cause, they can reassure themselves when they look at the text-books of the sciences or the edicts of a Marxian State.

While examining commonly used words which come from the ancient Greek mythology as well as the ancient Greek science, I found myself renewing my old habit of looking in astonishment and curiosity at words which I had taken for granted without any query as to the whence and wherefore. Why, for example, are people described as cantankerous? This was a word which I had just been using in an article: but I could not explain it without turning to the dictionary and, when I have turned to the dictionary, I cannot easily get out of it. In a world much exposed to writers specializing in anger it seemed worth while to do some brief research into cantankeriety.

Furthermore, the oddities of modern usage in the gossip columns, general reporting and caption-writing of the newspapers began to force me back into my hobby of word-collection. Accordingly my notes and comments began shaping themselves into another book and involved me once more in breach of promise. Having said (or written) my Last Word and then broken it, I was at it again.

There is this excuse. The new book differs from those in my previous Word Series since it is hardly at all concerned with the rescue of amusing and attractive words. I had finished my anthologies: this time it was not the flowers of the dictionary, but the freaks and weeds that I was sorting out. What I have tried is simple interpretation for a puzzled public and not valuation for those who have read much and would enjoy more. None the less, I hope that the latter class, whose members have so kindly followed and so largely assisted my meanderings among words in the past, assisting, indeed, to the point of almost writing my books for me, will find something of interest or amusement in this further excursion.

I would like once again to thank my many correspondents: often they send questions which I cannot answer with confidence; often they send suggestions which I can follow up with pleasure. Some write from far-away places: it seems that the English language begets increased affection and stimulates a livelier curiosity when seen from a distance. Others are fascinated by the devices of journalism to find new verbal ways of seeming urgent and up to the minute. In this connection I am particularly indebted to Sir Linton Andrews, the Editor of the *Yorkshire Post* and Chairman of the Press Council, for his pamphlet on Newspaper English. He amusingly shows that usages for which journalists are blamed occur amid the splendours of the Authorized Version of the Bible. The mysteries of Headline English are also shrewdly explored. Perhaps, observing the idiom, I should describe this section of Sir Linton's essay as 'Press Boss Caption Probe'.

WORDS IN OUR TIME

ADDICT

WE hear much of addicts in these times. The word fits the increasing tendency of the age to treat crime or vice as a symptom of disease or as a misfortune of the maladjusted. (See note on Maladjusted in due course.) We must be merciful. To call a man an addict of alcohol is much kinder than to call him a sot, soak, or deplorable drunkard. In the same way a glutton is let off lightly if he is described as an addict of good feeding. There is in London a Society for the Study of Addiction, whose guest I have happily been. I may add that I was not invited as an exhibit, whose remarkable case-sheet, abounding in frailties, merited the scrutiny of the assorted specialists, including doctors, psychologists and lawyers engaged in the observation and treatment of human weakness. The subject offers a wide range of oddity in taste and temptation. I felt that if I were in one of those professions, I might easily become an addict of addiction-study.

Addict is a well-established term. Falstaff observed: 'If I had a thousand sons the first humane principle I would teach them should be to forswear thin potations and addict themselves to sack.' Thin potations he had previously dismissed as the companions of many fish-meals and coolness of blood: their addicts, in his opinion, fall into a green-sickness and get wenches when they marry. Falstaff's one-time comrade in revel and a fellow 'minion of the moon', Prince Hal, was described by the then Archbishop of Canterbury as 'an addict of vain courses', since his hours were filled up with riots, banquets and sports, and his nature was unstudious and too solid to endure any retirement or sequestration. Another Shakespearian addict was Laertes, of whom his father Polonius asked Reynaldo to say that 'he's very wild, addicted so and so'. The vagueness of 'so-and-so' is charming. Addiction-observers of today could probably be more precise and bring out a resounding and polysyllabic classical name for whatever addictions were being imputed to Laertes by that fuss-pot and chatter-box parent with an ugly addiction to spying on his children.

One can, I suppose, be called an addict of the mildest pleasures. The width of usage allows us to be addicts of anything from a cup of tea to a debauch of drugs. The employment of this gentle term helps to destroy the atmosphere of melodrama which not long ago surrounded the pursuit of tranquillity through dope. The elegant and briskly social ladies in Ouida's novels took ether as a tranquil-lizer; the mid-Victorians were used to the absorption of laudanum by their poets, and when Sir Arthur Conan Doyle first invented Sherlock Holmes, he made his hero an addict of cocaine injections; Doyle, who was a doctor, evidently believed that a few jabs at moments of excessive strain did no harm.

But soon after that public opinion began to be worked up by hysterical declamation against all opiates. Doyle henceforward omitted the cocaine, leaving Holmes to find his solace in heavy pipe-smoking and rapt application to his violin. At this period takers of drugs were labelled dope-fiends and it was generally conveyed to the young that the slightest addiction to a stimulant or a tranquillizing drug was a step on the road to moral ruin and physical collapse.

We no longer discuss surrender to the herbs and liquors that ease man's life with so vehement a use of vocabulary. It is true that the law against the importing and sale of drugs is strict; but we do not call up terrifying pictures of delirium tremens to frighten the drinker, nor do we scream 'Fiend!' in the face of anyone who prefers hemp to tobacco in his cigarettes. We murmur the word 'addiction' sympathetically and murmur also that a soul-doctor might find the way out.

ADLIBBING

To adlib has become a verb in English usage; authority may not acknowledge it, but most people who do any speaking or broadcasting know what it means. *Ad lib* was the shortened form of the Latin *ad libitum*, meaning 'to one's pleasure'. Since the Latin *libertas* and our liberty both begin with lib, it was naturally thought that speaking *ad lib* meant speaking freely, without censorship. But that is a mistake.

Ad lib was at one time chiefly used as an addition to helping yourself, and here again the idea of freedom was involved. 'Help yourself *ad lib*' meant, properly, take, eat, or drink as much as you want or can cram in. Speaking *ad lib* should mean 'talk as much as you like'. But nowadays it has come to mean improvising. When a talker has a written speech or script for broadcasting he may be told to 'adlib a bit', in order to give an impression of freshness and spontaneity. The adlibber in the theatre is one who introduces what are called 'gags', that is lines invented by himself. Shakespeare, through the mouth of Hamlet, said, 'Let those who play your clowns speak no more than is set down for them' and scolded his comedians for holding up 'some necessary question of the play' by interpolated jests and by laughing at their own jokes. In this he was denouncing, as an aggrieved author, the adlibbers of the stage who were winning laughter to their own pleasure and to his vexation. He wanted them to speak *ad hoc*, i.e. strictly to the object or purpose.

I have never heard the participle adhocking: but an adhocker, a sticker to the point, is often more valuable in discussion than even the most amusing adlibber. A bad adlibber is a dreadful nuisance.

To lib in rural English is to castrate and obviously has nothing to do with freedom or pleasure.

ADVENTURIST

WHEN Marshal Zhukov was sacked by his civilian boss, Mr Khruschev, he was formally accused of being adventurist and personalist. These words, of course, were the English translation of Russian adjectives, but they will probably pass into the jargon of British Communism and rank with its other pet terms such as liquidate for murder and realistic for any form of intolerant cruelty. Individualist now sounds rather stodgy and Victorian, and in a world where the personality of the charmers and entertainers is so constantly 'plugged' a personalist, as a variant from egoist and exhibitionist, seems to be justified.

But what is meant by Adventurist? To a Briton it would seem to be a complimentary term, but the Briton lives in a society which retains some remnants of regard for freedom and the taking of chances. In a society of forced equality (or supposed equality) the adventurist is putting out his neck: he is soon regarded as a traitor: and the necks of traitors have always been their danger-points. Meanwhile we can return to our own national history with lively gratitude for the appearance therein of a number of personalists and adventurists. *Heroes and Hero-worship* was, whether you share Carlyle's taste in heroes or not, a better title than *Adventurists and Addicts of Adventurism*.

AMAZON

WHILE I was gazing at my television screen, I saw a play about a girl who was embarrassed by being so tall. One of the characters said of her: 'She's gawky. She's an Amazon.' After that she was alluded to as 'The Amazon'.

The South American Amazon is a very long river, but the lanky lady was not thus described from considerations of geography and riparian length. Geography does, however, come into it. The original Amazons, extremely bellicose females, were first on the rampage in ancient Greek mythology. It was believed by the Greeks that the women of Asia Minor, who inhabited the shores of the Black Sea, were uncommonly fierce and formidable and could take on even the sturdiest of menfolk with a sword or even an axe. So the legends multiplied of Warrior Women who used to go raiding the areas ruled by men and scaring the poor males out of their tunics.

Swinging down from their native haunts the legendary Amazons practised invasion on a large scale. It needed the great Achilles himself to cope with Penthesilea, Queen of the Amazons. Theseus, the mythical saviour of ancient Athens in times of stress, was called on to rid Attica of these intrusive feminine swarms. The mighty Heracles (Hercules), he who coped with every kind of monster, hydra-headed serpent, colossal crabs, the Nemean lion, human giants, Cretan bull, wild oxen, ferocious stag and the rest, practised counter-invasion in order to steal the girdle of Hippolyta, Queen of the Amazons. He had to fight her for it and succeeded in killing her.

The conflict of Achilles and Penthesilea was a favourite theme of ancient sculptors. A sarcophagus discovered at Salonica presents Achilles raising the body of his dying opponent, who appears to have discarded a breastplate and fought naked except for a Phrygian peaked cap and top-boots. The man had no unfair advantage of armour: he had only his helmet and no footwear. But the general tradition of the myths made Amazons wear the trousers, like any modern housewife doing her suburban shopping.

We come across one of the Amazon monarchs in Shakespeare; Duke Theseus in *A Midsummer Night's Dream* married Queen Hippolyta, whom we meet with her Spartan hounds in the hunting-field. It was gallant of him to take this party into such close partner-ship, for she is described as

<blockquote>
the bouncing Amazon,
Your buskin'd mistress and your warrior love.
</blockquote>

So she wore the boots, carried the spear, and bounced into the

B

bargain. Thoughts of our modern stage suggest for the part Miss Tessie O'Shea, known as 'two-ton Tessie', instead of the slender beauties usually cast for this role.

The notion of great height in Amazons continued to abide in balladry.

> Old Meg was brave as Margaret Queen
> And tall as Amazon.

The Amazons of our time, the women members of the three armed forces, are by no means Amazonians of the classic stature and temper. To stimulate recruiting in peace-time it is necessary to provide uniforms which will be as feminine as possible. The Wren can be as *petite* as her avian namesake. Bouncing and booted warrior-women remain only in the picture-gallery of the myths.

ANTIPODES

WHY Antipodes for territories in the Southern Hemisphere? Because, by Greek derivation, this means 'foot against foot'. We in the North have our feet on the ground: our friends in the South are naturally posed likewise. But, because they are on the other side of a globular world, their feet are pointing upwards by our reckoning, and so, in a topsyturvy way, we are foot against foot, with the force of gravity to make sense of the contradiction. In older English usage 'to be in antipodes' meant to be in strong contrast. 'Fools are in antipodes to the wise.' Fortunately the cosmic scheme keeps the Antipodeans and ourselves equally erect. So the Australians are just as much Antipodean to us as we are to them.

Another word used in these reckonings is Hyperborean. This, by another Greek derivation, means 'beyond the north wind'. The ancient Greeks believed that, when you got beyond that icy blast, all was very well indeed and that a land of sunshine and plenty awaited those who broke the wind-barrier and were really on top of the world. Our Polar explorers at both ends of the world long ago shattered that hopeful fancy. But the inhabitants of the Anti-podean lands, provided they do not go too far south, may have the radiance and riches so queerly attributed to the Hyperboreans. Yet they do not have so much riches or fun or benefit of sunshine if they happen to be scratching a living in the Central Australian desert, where 'falls not hail or rain or any snow', but where dust storms abound and water has to be watched and saved, as a miser watches and treasures gold. Antipodean life is not all bathing in sun, surf and abundance of good things.

Another impressive term for northerners is Septentrionals, derived from the Seven Stars of the Great Bear. Shakespeare (in the Third Part of *Henry VI*, I. iv.) used both Septentrion and Antipodes together.

> Thou art as opposite to every good
> As the Antipodes are unto us,
> Or as the South to the Septentrion.

Benedick in *Much Ado About Nothing* 'rather than hold three words conference with that harpy' (Beatrice) said that he would fetch a tooth-picker from the furthest inch of Asia or 'go on the slightest journey to the Antipodes you can resolve to send me on'.

When did our geographers first discover that we of the Septen-trion are really standing foot to foot with the Antipodeans?

ASPECTED

THE advices of our Fleet Street star-gazers appear to be widely studied and enjoyed. Even a paper of such quality as the *News Chronicle* thinks it prudent to include the familiar horoscopic jottings. Its expert on stellar influences, Mr Leon Petulengro, is doubtless a reliable judge of what is celestially cooking and I am 'all eyes' for his prognostication of what is coming my way. He employs a remarkable language which has its own fascination.

Having been born under the Sign of the Bull, I naturally watch my immediate destiny and that of my fellow Taurines. I learned that for us, during a certain week: 'Journeys, social and home affairs are well aspected.' This type of reassurance should improve my own aspect with a confident smile when I buy a ticket or fix up a visit.

Another astrological favourite is Trend. For the Capricorners in the same week Mr Petulengro has the good news: 'Social trends show up well in your off-duty hours.' I observe that trend is a great help to women journalists writing about 'haute couture'. The words fashion, mode and vogue are so heavily worked that trend comes in as a useful reserve. Paris, it seems, abounds in trends for the devotees of elegance. Now, in my off-duty hours, I shall soon expect my own 'social trends' to show up well, since the Capricorners cannot have all the fun and the Taurines must have their turn. What exactly are 'social trends'? They will include, I am sure, attendance at a well-aspected party.

AUDIOPHILE

I owe this word to Dr H. Angus Bowes of McGill University and to Toronto's *Saturday Night*, in which review the doctor's opinions on 'The Psychopathology of Hi-Fi Addicts' were recorded. (Hi-Fi is short for High Fidelity.) Dr Bowes began by affirming 'as emphatically and categorically as I may that I do not consider that the enjoyment of recorded music is in itself any indication of abnormality or psychopathological disturbances'.

So far, so cautious. The doctor then distinguished between the audiophile who 'appreciates recorded music in an intelligent and controlled manner' and the confirmed Hi-Fi addict, who appears to be a species of masochist, glorying in his own distress. 'For him the sound must be turned up until it reaches the physical level of pain; each of the instruments must stand out so that the tinkle of a triangle sounds like the clanging of a fire-bell, the contra-bassoon sounds like a foghorn, and the percussion department like a boiler-factory.' While the audiophile discreetly turns his knobs, the addict seeks in Hi-Fi 'loud aggressive passages of orgiastic violence' and not only finds them but distributes them to the agony of all his tranquilly audiophilous neighbours.

This brought protest from the Hi-Fi-Faithful. Dr Bowes was denounced as 'head shrinker', whatever that may be, and the whole profession of psychiatrists was dismissed as 'screw-ball'. It appears that Hi-Fi addicts are shy of psychotherapy, even when they have reached the stage of wanting only recorded noises, such as those of railway trains and thunderstorms, and will have no music at all. Having some modern music in mind we may doubt whether there is much difference between the two: the addict who differentiates is being fussy as well as frantic.

One encouraging fact emerged from this 'stramash'. Very few women are Hi-Fi addicts: few, oddly, are even audiophiles. It can, of course, be unkindly suggested that women resent the various kinds of recorded melody as well as of maniacal din because they have a strong wish to speak and to be heard. The Hi-Fi addict, on the other hand, has nothing to say and silently enjoys his immersion in uproar. Should a psychotherapist put his 'snoot' round the door, the addict will be delighted to do a bit of banging.

Writing as a modest audiophile, I realize that I have been warned.

AUDITIONED

'FIVE hundred applicants for the London chorus of the great Broadway musical *The King and She*, based on Shakespeare's *King Lear* were personally auditioned by the director, Hyman Sam-burger.' This sort of paragraph is part of my daily reading. Of course, to audition a young lady whose looks are her glory is absurd. Surely it is the eye of Mr Samburger that must be enchanted, not his ear; he knows his public and it wants an eyeful. Furthermore, the cumbrous turning of noun into verb is another absurdity.

An Audit was originally a judicial hearing of complaints and then an inquiry into debts, followed, it was hoped, by a settlement thereof. In acknowledging, or hoping for, friendlier relations the landlord, either having received his rents or eager to stimulate his tenants into paying them, entertained them to Audit Dinners. The great office building, Bush House, in Aldwych, London, gave until recently an Audit Lunch to its tenants at Christmas time. The Audit Ale once brewed at Colleges was famous for quality and power. Financial inquiry is not synonymous with meanness in one party or distress in the other. But with the word audit having these various financial and social meanings we cannot, as was said, audit the potential cast of a play.

Hence the foolish-looking verb 'to audition', which draws on the word audience rather than on the word audit. Kings give audience and listen to what is said. Theatrical directors give audience to aspiring performers and may be more eagerly estimating appearances and watching dances than giving ear to the noises made. To audition a ballet dancer seems a particularly ridiculous way of speaking. But young players of all kinds no longer go up to be tested. They must be auditioned, even if they are to be cast as mutes.

AUTOCUE

THIS sounds like a labour-saving device at the billiard-table. The player would get his weapon properly poised and after that it would be what is now called 'a press-button job'. The shaky or uncertain hand could not frustrate the intended master-stroke.

But the autocue is, in fact, one of the gadgets introduced by television. The speaker or recorder of news has in front of him a screen over which his text passes. Thus he can read without looking down or fidgeting with papers. Actors on the stage, when afflicted with bad memory or called on to play a part at short notice, have had various devices for having bits of the dialogue available in odd corners of the furniture. It needed great skill to snatch glimpses at these reminders without seeming to do so. An autocue in the prompter's corner would be helpful, but would necessitate either very long sight, the sudden use of spectacles, or great neatness in getting within viewing range without disturbing the positions and upsetting the balance of the other actors. To be a television narrator, using the autocue without seeming to use it and staring fixedly at the screen, also demands considerable address.

AUTOMATION

WE have been hearing much of automation. It has seemed to me a vague term as well as a vogue term and I was glad to have the reassuring support of Lord Halsbury who, as the managing director of the National Research Development Corporation, speaks with knowledge and authority. In an interview he explained that Automation started as a slang word in the Ford Works at Detroit. Accused of going round and lecturing on Automation, he explained that in fact he went round telling people that it didn't mean anything. If a machine produces one piece of machinery and that piece is automatically fed to another, then, he explained, there is a sequence of machine operations that is called Transfer Machining. This process is more than thirty years old; it began in Britain, at the Morris Motor Works, in 1923. The modern factory in some of its departments achieves what is properly described as Flow-Production. Lord Halsbury maintained that we can call transfer machining a flow-production automation if we like, but he didn't see that anything was gained by use of a term which suggests something new when there is nothing really new.

However, I do not suppose that people will be deterred from talking about automation, which is less clumsy than automatization. The word is pleasantly pompous for those who enjoy a little verbal display and it calls up rich visions of Progress, progress towards a wonderful world which will continuously be giving us more and more for less and less. Whether complete automation can automatically produce such 'joy in widest commonalty spread' remains to be seen.

BAFFLEGAB

HERE is a plain term used by Americans as an alternative to Gobbledygook; both describe the monstrous and mystifying language in which official documents are written. My own term for this has been the Barnacular, based on the Dickensian family of Tite Barnacles who clung with such tenacity to official posts. The Barnacles were really the forerunners (or, more accurately, forestickers) of what is now called 'The Establishment', i.e. the group of families who, without ostensibly holding much power, are in fact very influential behind the scenes. They have a tradition of getting their relations into jobs that matter while they themselves remain behind the political scene when they are not in them. They do not speak bafflegab, perhaps, but, in the way of all politicians they must learn and practise the tricky evasive style now known as double-talk.

I am informed by reference to my *Dictionary of New Words* that the term Gobbledygook was invented by Maury Maverick of Texas: Miss Reifer, compiler of this work, does not attribute Bafflegab to any particular creator or State of the Union. Whoever did first exclaim in anger, 'Sheer bafflegab!' when confronted with a new form written in officialese, had a good idea of a descriptive and dismissive noun. We might marry the two nicknames and talk of Bafflegabbledygook, but the short and expressive bafflegab is good enough for me.

BEANLESS

'SORRY, I'm beanless', I heard a young woman remark when there was some question of expenditure. The bean, to be precise, is the 'smooth, kidney-shaped seed of a leguminous plant', which does not sound exciting. But the uses of it in slang are none the less numerous; they are also strangely contradictory.

Bean, for example, ranks with loaf, napper and others as slang for head. One can be dotted on the bean. In the works of P. G. Wodehouse to be beaned is to be hit on the head. So the adjective beany might mean clever: but it is applied to the blood, not the brain. In the stables beany means spirited, because a bean-fed horse is likely to be skittish. Yet, 'giving them beans', as applied to human beings, is unkindly and does not suggest giving them a gastronomic treat. I surmise that the introduction of beans in this phrase to signify 'socking them hard' is based on the dreariness of a diet of dried beans, a fact grimly familiar to soldiers and sailors short of other vegetables. Savourless and windy, dried beans are fit only to be counters in family games. On the table they offer a diet for which, in another sense, one would not give a row of beans. A very old English writer rightly observed, 'Beans are harde of digestion and make troblesome dreames.' Yet a bean-feast indicates a good tuck-in and one does not expect 'hard tack' when offered a beano.

So we have this queer confusion. A bean is a symbol of the headpiece in man, of energy in horses, of vigour in punishment, and of worthlessness in property, as in the case of our beanless miss and other persons and articles 'not worth a row of beans'. It signifies both austerity and luxury in feeding. Bean, for money, refers, I suppose, to small coins. To be beanless is to lack even a copper. Yet one can call a companionable codger 'quite a nice old bean'. What puzzles me is why English-speaking man, in his colloquial use of words, has been so much and so variously fascinated by this 'seed of a leguminous plant'.

BLISTER AND OTHERS

THE vocabulary of abuse and denigration, some of it genial and some of it sardonic, has had its fascinating changes within a decade or two. Words like blighter and perisher have become faded and old-fashioned: we are now intensely clinical in our language of personal derision and contempt. We deal rather in scars and swellings. Clot, blot, boil and blister have replaced the perishing blighter.

The one-time twerp, admirable but out of date, was a term of uncertain origin. It now seems to carry the look of 1930. But I am glad to see it when it occasionally reappears. The creature in question is, with less grace, more often described in our time as an ulcer, sore, wart, or drip. Or else 'the man's a pill'. That pill should be included in these ugly dismissals seems to me foolish since a pill is very easy to swallow and should have lightening, and even lightning, results. Pills are now many in kind. The globule may be a stimulant as well as a valuable purge or soothing tranquillizer. I should consider myself flattered if called a pill. A blister is not at all so kindly. American fiction contributes the horrid little word fink for a person of the blisterish kind. Hence, I suppose, that twerpish and blottish Wodehouse character, Gussie Fink-Nottle, who is described, I think, as 'Britain's major wart'.

To dismiss a person as a pain-in-the-neck is to give a modest description of the offensive type and the phrase is now almost an antique. Our period demands something more vividly repulsive and draws on the vocabulary of streptococcic infection, a filthy form of plague.

Most foods are welcome and so they are used to flatter and cajole. Honey, sugar and sweetie-pie are natural synonyms for a dear one. There is no reason to employ larder language for purposes of condemnation. Tripe, which, stewed with milk and onions and served with mashed or baked potato, can, for some people, be an estimable slop. But it is relegated to the ranks of blots and clots, having been made the common synonym for rubbish in argument and for trash in writing. I have seen a twerpish type called a piece of cheese, presumably because cheese, in a prolonged maturity, can be malodorous. But this is unfair to a noble aliment (crossword-puzzle English for food) and we should greatly honour a blister if we called him a portion of Port Salut.

Slang is particularly unfair to fish. We hear of Poor Fish, but never of Fine Fish. Does one think appraisingly of hake or haddock? The nimble and elegant trout had its justified place in G. M. Hopkins's list of dappled beauties. He sang of 'rose-moles all in stipple upon trout that swim' along with 'skies of couple-colour' and finches' wings. Yet we constantly demean this tasty as well as decorative creature by adding the adjective old and by describing an elderly, stolid and generally unpleasing human being as an old trout. I have also noted old prawn derisively employed. Injustice again. Since scampi are so fashionable on the menu, to be unkind to prawns is illogical and absurd.

Fruits, lemons excluded, are kindly employed. Even the prune, so long the jocose title for a mutt, mug, or duffer, has come to enjoy kindly usage, at least as applied to a girl. 'A sweet little prune' suggests that the dried plum is now attaining the lofty valuation of a fresh peach. Trees, on the other hand, are regarded as the source of thorns in the flesh and of silly chumps. A vegetable chump is, or was, a log of wood and must not be confused with the animal chump, signifying the better kind of mutton-chop, less loaded with wasteful fat than the loin-chop.

Pansy, which seems to have taken up permanent residence in our verbal flower-bed as a substitute for cissy, is one of the few blossoms condemned to keep company with the drips and blisters.

BROOKING

THE noun brook is a break and therefore an outburst, especially of water, and so a spring or a stream. In the lyricism of popular songs the brook is generally babbling. Brook as a verb has a quite different meaning and, though it sounds and looks simple enough, it has become one of the words only met with in Leading Articles and Letters to the Editor. These have a jargon of their own. For example, I have noticed that, in a letter to *The Times* written by the Dean of Canterbury praising the estimable qualities of education in Soviet Russia, there was a final exhortation to Great Britain to wake up and do likewise. The Dean ended with the statement that such reform 'brooks no delay'.

This use of brook is Miltonic: 'Heaven', said that poet, 'brooks not the works of violence and war', a line possibly unknown to the Soviet Commissars who, in any case, are less concerned with heaven than is the Dean. But how deep is the rift between 'Letters to the Editor' English and our ordinary domestic speech! Do any normal folk, do even deans in their deaneries, say, 'The roof is leaking. Repair brooks no delay'? Brooking of this kind, i.e. putting up with, is usually associated by writers of editorial letters and leading articles with interference and delay. One always imagines that a scribe who will brook neither of these is puffing rather heavily and pressing on his pen. Perhaps this business of no-brooking is one of the reasons why the nibs of the pens in hotels especially catering for retired admirals and generals are always in a crossed or crushed condition. Yet none of these vessels of wrath would say to the waitress in the hotel dining-room that the soup is stone-cold again, a matter no longer to be brooked.

Sir Winston Churchill, with his famous relative clause, 'up with which I will not put', was certainly using more syllables than if he had refused to brook the objectionable article. But he was avoiding the kind of language which deserves a name of its own. What shall it be? Leaderese?

BUILD-UP

THIS has now become 'officialese' for any kind of growth and increase. Its meaning is obvious: there is no bafflegab here. But its use is often silly. Here is a typical piece of pomposity from a

Government Department. Concerning an epidemic, this announcement was made:

> There is now evidence of some spread in the population locally, but no evidence at present of any large build-up. The possibility of the infection becoming widespread later cannot be ruled out.

This can be translated, with economy, 'The infection is spreading a little locally, and may increase'.

'Cannot be ruled out', as a gaseous synonym for 'possible', has become a great favourite among our Public Relations Officers and has found its way into journalism of all kinds. The chance that a monarch might lose his throne would certainly appear in print in some such form as this: 'The possibility of King Hasbîn ceasing to maintain his rule in Pseudo-Arabia cannot be ruled out.'

Build-up should surely suggest purpose. One naturally visualizes that an architect is at work. Are we to imagine some master-builder of bacilli planning an extension of the epidemic?

Build-up, as another word for growth, might be ruled out altogether.

BUMS AND BUMMAREES

WE all know that people are very touchy about their professional names. Who now, in need of domestic help, would dare to advertise for a cook-general? If such a treasure is to be engaged at all, House-keeper she must be. Are there shop-walkers still? Sales Superintendents do their job. Any master of any craft, however simple, has to be nominated an Expert. 'Lettuces should be well washed before using them in salads', said a Domestic Science Expert. The rat-catcher's social grading as a Rodent Officer has been respected for some time.

Accordingly, one may surmise that the old bum-bailiff has now become a Debt-Recovery Commissioner. The Bailiff was just a general term for holders of high office, including mayors and sheriffs. They had their dominions known as bailiwicks. The bum-bailiff, as the prefix announces, was in a lower order of our Civil Service, and harassed debtors, visited by bum-bailiffs for removal of their property, naturally liked to emphasize the word bum and to dismiss the legal invaders of their homes as bums and no more. John Galsworthy in his play *The Pigeon* introduced three characters called Humblemen who were doing the bum-bailiff's work. I have not seen or heard that word elsewhere. Was the term bum reached by a slurring abbreviation of these courteously entitled Humble-men?

The bum-boats of the harbour also started in a humble way: they were engaged in collecting filth and refuse from the vessels in port. Later they were freed from squalor and became the floating barrows of fruit and vegetable sellers, renewing ships' stores with valuable preventives of scurvy.

The American 'bum' is a tramp and may be ragged and hungry. No wonder, then, that the so-called 'bummarees' engaged in por-ters' work at Smithfield protested not long ago that the term was 'obnoxious'. They conceived the label to be one that bumped or 'bummed' them into the lowest possible class. But they need not have been so fussy. The word is a veteran with eighteenth-century usage and dictionary status to give it dignity.

There were 'bummarees' at Billingsgate in 'Good King George's Golden Days' (George III, that is) and they plainly were not at the bottom of the market's social register. The bummarees were then middle-men in the fish trade, and middle-men do not, as a rule, starve or go in danger of the law's invading 'bums'. But how they came by this bummarious title, nobody seems to know.

BY T'WALLOP

WALLOP has many meanings. I like the old Yorkshire one signifying lump, mass or dollop. This usage still qualifies, I am glad to hear, for entry in a book on words in our time: but only just, for it would be exceptional now to hear it said, even in Yorkshire, that a gossiping chatter-box talks 'by t'wallop'. A rough job was called 'done by t'wallop' and a rough calculation was also a 'by t'wallop' job. The correspondent who reminded me of this also mentioned 'getting their onions' as a phrase for being reprimanded or 'being told off'. A man engaged on a delicate job who did it 'by t'wallop' could 'get his onions' from the foreman or boss. Nowadays 'carpeting' appears to be the favourite term in the lingo of administration. A broad-caster who had made an error of judgment, as his superiors thought, told the Press that he had not been 'carpeted'. But it certainly seemed that he had received onions 'by t'wallop' from someone on high.

CANTANKEROUS

THERE is certainly nothing topical about the word Cantankerous. I mention it because I suddenly found myself staring at it and won-dering how this odd adjective got there. This staring at words which one commonly uses is a habit which leads to astonishment and so to entertaining as well as instructive research. For example, I have just used the word topical with the meaning of contemporary. But the Greek, topos, meant a place and topography is still the practice of mapping or describing places. Why should topical mean anything more than local? In its meandering history the topic, after becoming a theme discussed in a certain place, especially the scholas-tic premises of Aristotle, lost the idea of place altogether and became a subject of discussion. Then, because subjects of discussion are often the affairs of our own time, the adjective topical moved from the geographical world to the chronological. So when I wrote 'nothing topical' in my first sentence, I might have written more simply nothing of our period, or nothing new. It is often rewarding, for those with any curiosity about words, to look at terms in con-stant use as if one were seeing them for the first time. Those who do so will receive some shocks, so often do we employ words with no knowledge of their origin or history.

Back to cantankerous. Having written of some character in a play that he was cantankerous, I was puzzled by the look of this adjective. Can and Tank suggested liquidity, but liquor, though it may make people cantankerous, is not necessarily implied. The most abstemious can be surly, tetchy and combative.

So to the dictionary, which tells me of an old English word contak, meaning strife. Hence came an adjective, contakerous meaning quarrelsome. But then confusion of sound, which often has much to do with our word-making, entered in. There was rancorous for embittered. So, by a fortunate muddle, we got the expressive cantankerous, which makes the right noise for a description of testy and truculent folk.

It was employed at one time to suggest harsh things as well as prickly persons. Oliver Goldsmith wrote, concerning a rough journey in times when ways were horrid with stones or foul with mud, 'there's not a more bitter, cantanckerous road in all Christendom'. Pedestrians, cyclists, horsemen and motorists may all have been grateful in their time for that adjective. Those exploring the North and West Highlands of Scotland may find that it well suits both the track and traveller at journey's end. Furthermore, the miserable inadequacy of our congested main roads from England to Scotland, whose well-kept surface is no compensation for their narrowness and curving nature over many miles, may well produce extremely cantankerous drivers after some hours of frustrated incarceration behind a string of gigantic lorries and trucks.

In one of the excellent murder-stories by Ngaio Marsh, which usually mingle ingenuity of crime-plot with much learning in the arts — Old English folk plays in the case of this one, *Off With His Head* — I came across a rustic version of cantankerous. This was cranktankerous — and it admirably suited the author's German folklorist at large in our shires, Mrs Bunz, who became almost frenzied in her fanatical search for the remnants of ancient ritual. She was indeed a cranktankerous party.

CEREBROTONIC

THIS formidable polysyllable received Parliamentary honours not long ago. Being puzzled by it, I wrote to the Member who used it in the House of Commons to ask what he meant by it. My own mind had been working this way. Cerebrum is the Latin for brain and the word tonic is usually employed as a noun to mean a strengthener or stimulant. So I thought that the Member had been referring to some brain-quickening drug. But I was wrong. He explained to me that he had in mind one whose brain is stretched too tight and who is therefore 'a hypersensitive intellectual'. Tonic is an adjective as well as a noun and originally it meant 'pertaining to tension'. Cerebrotonics, accordingly, are not tots to drink for mental 'pep' but types who need to be calmed down if the over-taut fabric of their brains seems near to snapping. To high-brows we must now add tight-brows.

> When the mental strain is chronic
> You are deemed cerebrotonic.
> Hear the psychopathic moan
> Of the glum cerebrotone,
> Pouring guineas in the fist
> Of a psycho-therapist,
> Crying, 'Oh, sir, have you got any
> Cure for raging cerebrotony?'

The healer thus approached might observe that mental oddity was once described in terms of a screw loose: but now it is not slackness in the skull but tension of intellectual screwing that gets the blame. A possible remedy for cerebrotony might, therefore, be going on the loose.

The phrase 'getting tight' for intoxication has always seemed to me absurd. The function of the grape and grain, suitably treated, is not to tighten us up but to ease and liberate. It will more probably lead to laxity of behaviour than to strictness of standards. Those 'on the bottle' are more often 'on the loose' than seeking to be straitened in the working of the mind and code of morals. So the cerebrotones may reasonably consider a moderate application to alcohol as the best antidote to their excessive tension.

Since writing that note I have learned more about cerebrotonics. They are 'usually of ectomorphic body-build', which means that they have 'long, fragile body-bones and a highly developed nervous system, lying, as it were, with little protection by other tissues'. (*A Dictionary of New English.*) The possession of lengthy and brittle bones, together with much-developed and much-exposed nerves, creates a type, according to the same authority, which 'prefers solitude, is intent and ambitious and inclined towards timidity'. It is sad that intently ambitious people should also be shy of company and apprehensive. This must make the achievement of their ambitions very difficult and produce the painful tensions of Cerebrotony.

CHAR

THE charwoman owns distinguished ancestry and has her place in Shakespeare, being alluded to by Cleopatra herself: 'The maid that milks and does the meanest chares.' We have turned chares, jobs of work, into chores, but the charwoman has kept the letter 'a'.

Naturally, Mrs Mop likes a cup of char, modern slang for tea, to ease the passage of the day. It is unlikely that Civil Servants, with a great legendary reputation as char-consumers, are more absorbent than the rest of us. My own observation of the building trade at work is that its operatives — sometimes a courtesy title — are more frequently stopping for a 'cuppa' than any other brand of contemporary toiler.

Char, our slang for 'the cups that cheer but not inebriate' is more common in speech than in print and, when printed, carries a final 'r'. But it should be cha, which is Chinese. So is our tea, taken from the Chinese (t'e), Amoy dialect. Char, with us, is proletarian slang, but the Chinese cha was a Mandarin's word and therefore more aristocratic than t'e.

Tea-drinking in England began in the middle of the seventeenth century. It was an enormously expensive habit, for the leaf cost as much as 30s. a pound, a gigantic sum then. Pepys spelled it tee, which suggests that it was so pronounced at first. Was it 'refanement' that turned it into tay?

> Here, thou, great Anna, whom three realms obey,
> Dost sometimes Counsel take — and sometimes tea.

It is unlikely that Pope pronounced obey as obee.

We had Chinese teas, tees, or tays for two centuries before we took to the stronger, darker and cheaper Indian and Ceylon teas. The average domestic worker would not thank her employer for a cup of the Mandarin's cha. She wants her 'elevenses' to be a more potent pick-me-up, that is to say a good black cup of char, which I have heard described, perhaps with menacing accuracy, as stomach-stain. A glance at the side of the cup sometimes confirms that idea of gastric pigmentation.

The Victorians spoke of Cha, the best Chinese tea, as Twankai. Thackeray's characters sip a cup of Twankai, since that city gave its name to quality as regions do to wines. It seems that Twankai was turned, by less exalted persons, into Twanky. Hence the otherwise inexplicable Widow Twanky in pantomimes which use the Aladdin story and so have a Chinese setting. Twankies were tea-soaks and probably drank char, not cha.

There have been many, and not very successful, efforts to convert other nations from the pleasures of coffee (derived from an Arabic word) to those of tea-drinking. British, Irish and Australians have been the chief addicts of char and have generally preferred tea to coffee; but shortage of tea during war-time made many turn to coffee (in various forms) for their midday stimulation. By Dickens's time the democratic taste in England was for char and it was a dozen cups of that brew which set one of Mr Stiggins's admirers 'swellin' wisibly' before the eyes of Mr Weller.

Nowadays we do not bother about slow and careful infusion of our char. One brand is advertised as Quick Brew, implying that

no time is wasted. But our predecessors liked their tea to 'draw'
slowly. This leisurely preparation they called mashing.

CHEERYBYE

CHEERYBYE is really a more sensible form of saying farewell or
au revoir than the common cheerio. It introduces the parting note
of bye-bye to the good wishes for good fortune expressed in cheer.
It is most effective when used with the high-pitched East of Scotland
accent. I have heard Edinburgh girls cheerybyeing each other with
so fluting an intonation that I thought the word must be coming
out of the tops of their heads. In Glasgow, only forty miles away,
the intonation is vastly different. There I have heard cheerybye as
a chesty, or even gastric, rumble.

Adieu is now labelled 'archaism', which may be well since it is
unlikely to be properly pronounced. Our Shakespearian actors,
who ought to know better, will anglicize it shockingly — and so
murder the music of an exquisite grief. Consider the superb lines
of Troilus when parting must come.

> Injurious time now, with a robber's haste,
> Crams his rich thievery up, he knows not how.
> As many farewells as be stars in heaven
> With distinct breath and consign'd kisses to them,
> He fumbles up into a loose adieu
> And scants us with a single famish'd kiss,
> Distasted with the salt of broken tears.

I have heard the fifth line ended with a-Jew, just as I have heard,
at the Old Vic, jewel reduced to jool, with scansion and beauty
simultaneously ruined. If we cannot speak an adieu with a proper
acknowledgment of its original meaning, we had better put up
with the cheerios and cheerybyes of today.

CLAP-TRAP

I HAD thought clap-trap to be a fairly recent name for bosh. But, on looking it up, I found that it was used early in the eighteenth century. It is an accurate and expressive term for the kind of oratory which seeks to snare applause by its speciousness. Usually, clap-trap is applied to the writing or speaking of plausible rubbish. I was surprised to find it employed by Charlotte Brontë in the contemptuous dismissal of a painting. In *Villette* she described Lucy Snowe visiting a gallery and looking at a picture with much background detail and decoration. Lucy decided that 'while some of the details — as roses, gold cups, jewels, etc. — were very prettily painted, it was, on the whole, an enormous piece of clap-trap'.

Clap-trap has been superseded in our time by a number of Americanisms. I am now accustomed to boloney, presumably sausage-meat, and malarkey, whose origin is obscure. There are also the various forms of phoney, one of which 'the old phonus bolonus' (a Damon Runyon word) returns to Bologna and its famous botulistic product. Clap-trap has no mystery about it. It plainly means what it plainly says.

CLASSIC

IT goes back to the tax-gatherer. The first first class was a financial one. Servius Tullius, the sixth king of very ancient Rome, divided his people into six 'classes' — the plural is the same in Latin as in English — for purposes of making them pay their due or what he thought, and they probably did not think, was their due. Some Romans may not have wept when Servius was murdered by his son-in-law.

Since Latin became the universal language of Europe, the word classis or class spread widely. The Upper Class was at the top of society and the top of the school. Hence the 'U' talk we have heard so much about lately. Then classic became the adjective applied to the Greek and Roman languages. A classical education was one limited almost entirely to the study of these people, their tongues, literature, history and philosophy. This kind of training was called the Grand Old Fortifying Curriculum. To this I was myself submitted as a 'classical scholar' with the result that I left the University fortified to the young brim with ancient lore and a complete ignoramus about the world in which I was living. So I had to educate myself all over again.

Owing to the veneration of this curriculum, the word classic was applied to anything first-rate. Hence the Classic Races for three-year-old horses, victory in which carries substantial rewards and immense prestige. Now we speak of a classic whenever we mean something excellent in its kind, especially a long-established kind. Innovations acquire their classics in due course. *The Birth of a Nation* has been called a classic film, and I suppose Jazz has its classics by now.

The Socialists talk about creating a class-less society. But one thing about it is certain: it will not be tax-free. Servius Tullius had, as we say, 'started something'.

CLIFF-HANGER

I CAME across this word in a television studio. 'We've got a really good cliff-hanger', said a producer. What he meant was an effective end to an episode in a serial feature of the breath-taking kind. The typical cliff-hanger in these compositions provided a view of the hero grasping a cliff-top or ledge of a building and dangling in space: his coming move, up or down, was to be exhibited 'in our next'. So the word became a generic term for all such urgent incitements to 'read on from here' or 'look-in again next Thursday'.

A generation ago the supreme cliff-hanger was Harold Lloyd whose escapades on sky-scrapers were such dazzling displays of prehensile performance. The invisible Dick Barton was another artist in the provision of lethal crises on roof-tops. Suspensions in space, however, are not so common now as the finger on the trigger. Is the gun loaded? Will the aim be true? We may guess the answer with certainty: but we still want to know. Cliff-hanging is an undying exercise.

Shakespeare, when he brought the blinded Gloucester to the summit of the soaring cliffs of Dover, gave us the sheer poetry of cliff-suspension or rather of cliff-apprehension, since the old man was not bundled over.

> Hadst thou been aught but gossamer, feathers, air,
> So many fathom down precipitating,
> Thou'dst shiver like an egg: but thou dost breathe,
> Hast heavy substance: bleed'st not; speak'st; art sound.

The prospect of being dashed to smithereens and the avoidance of that fate does not often receive such language.

Why, incidentally, these mysterious smithereens? An Irish diminutive ending, we are told, has been added to smithers, which are fragments. But why should smithers describe fragmentation? Are they metal chippings, lying about in a smithy's workshop?

One of fiction's most famous feats of cliff-hanging was that of Sherlock Holmes on the rocks above the Reichenbach Falls, into which the body of Professor Moriarty, that monarch of the caco-demon world, had hurtled while his no less cacodemonic minister, Colonel Sebastian Moran, lurked above. 'It was not a pleasant business, Watson.' Holmes, of course, was always ready for a less unpleasant scramble on the tiles and over walls and for entry by window; a sill-hanger was one of his familiar antics. He even made Dr Watson an active scrambler over a six-foot wall when he burgled the lordly Hampstead home of Charles Augustus Milverton. But the Alpine energies above the Reichenbach chasm were surely the greatest of Holmes's achievements with the clutching hand and the finest proof of his steady head. He reached his goal, 'a ledge several feet deep and covered with green moss', where he evaded the nefarious Colonel's efforts to stone him. It is essential to the

best kind of cliff-hanger that the suspended victim should also be a
target for boulders or gun-fire.

That, indeed, was a blessed ledge as well as a blessed triumph for
Holmes's prehensile virtuosity. It brought him back from supposed
death to a myriad mourning readers of the *Strand Magazine* and
so provided the public with *The Return*, *His Last Bow* and the
Case Book, including thirty-five stories, twelve more than belong
to the pre-Reichenbach period. It was indeed a rewarding resur-
rection for the delectation of the Holmes addicts and for the pocket
of the author. But Conan Doyle lost in satisfaction what he gained
in purse. He much preferred writing other stories to devising new
problems for Holmes to cope with and new cliffs or ledges from
which he could suspend his tenacious hero.

Cliff-hangers will never cease, so long as serials are serials. The
heroes poised among Shakespeare's 'crows and choughs that wing
the mid-way air' are eternal hangers-on.

CLUE AND LABYRINTH

IT is natural to wonder what is the connection between these two.
If you are puzzled and if you also favour up-to-date jargon, you
will probably say that you 'haven't a clue'. A clue has now become
identical not only with a solution but also with any idea. I have just
read about a young lady, evidently a landlubber lass, who said:
'I'm clueless about sailing.' But in Shakespeare's time to say that
you hadn't a clue simply meant that you had not any thread or
string.

The old clew or clue was just that, a ball of thread. 'You have
wound a goodly clue', says Shakespeare's Countess of Rousillon
to Helena in *All's Well that Ends Well*. She meant that she had
created quite a tangle of affairs. The clue, as yarn, was tied up with
an ancient Greek legend about the Cretan Labyrinth. The latter
was a maze wherein dwelt a man-slaying monster called the Minotaur. The Greek hero Theseus managed to penetrate the Maze, kill

the Minotaur, and find his way out again. He was enabled to do this because of his fortunate endowment with sex-appeal. Ariadne, the daughter of the King of Crete, had fallen into love at first sight with Theseus. So she gave him a magic sword for slaughtering the beast and a clue or ball of thread to assist his escape from the Labyrinth. He unwound the clue as he went in and so had a trail to follow on his way out. During the eighteenth century the clue was used of other aids to coping with mysteries. Hence we reach the clues in a modern detective story or at the side of a crossword puzzle.

I had been doing crossword puzzles for years before I realized that my clues were really balls of thread. The old kind of clue could signify the whole ball and not the loosened thread. Very few people, I fancy, know this history of the helpful ball of string and of its contribution to our murder-mystery fiction and our daily sessions with the crossword setter's ingenious hints. If one of them chose to use the word labyrinth in his problem, he could fairly state in his clue-list that there's a clue to the clue here.

COPELESSNESS

'SHE suffers from copelessness.' I have heard this said of an un-satisfactory employee. The use of cope as a verb by itself to describe dealing with all kinds of situations is a recent usage. In my youth we tried, or were told to try, to cope with this or that problem. We were not required to cope in general.

To cope in Shakespeare's time was to strike (French, couper) or strike upon and so meet. The Banished Duke in *As You Like It* loved to cope with Jacques in his sullen fits, and Hamlet observed of his friend,

> Horatio, thou art e'en as just a man
> As e'er my conversation coped withal.

Cope could also be used with a sexual significance, as in 'Mis-Shapen Time, copesmate of ugly Night'. Iago persuaded the credulous Othello that Cassio had coped with Desdemona and would cope again.

Our coping is less carnal. We endeavour to cope with the cost of living; we are stricken with copelessness when confronted with Government forms loaded with the aforementioned bafflegab. Coping, in the sense of trading, has not quite vanished. Horse-coping is not, in a mechanized society, the commerce that it was, but most people know what manner of man a horse-coper might be. If in ignorance on the point, they can enjoyably meet him in full flavour by reference to Mr Soapey Sponge whose Sporting Tour Surtees so richly chronicled. Soapey, while coping with stable-finance, was by no means copeless.

The dealers' cope had a common English source in the cheaping (trading) which survives in Cheapside and in Chipping, prefix of several market-towns. The use of the adjective cheap to intimate a good deal for the purchaser seems to be an abbreviation of good cheap, the old English for a nice bargain. From the phrase cheap as dirt must have come the application of cheapness to one's physical condition. Those who say that they are feeling pretty cheap are on their way to the ancient accidie or slothful inertia, the state in which it is easy to be a victim of copelessness, should problems be thronging round.

COTCHELL

BUMMAREE, we gathered, was a word with an ancient and a fish-like smell. Cotchell, another piece of London market-language, is more fragrant. It belongs to Covent Garden and describes the bundle of vegetables which a porter can take away free. (Probably he says, 'I get it for free' nowadays.) Having been most of my life a journalist whose daily or nightly perquisite was only a copy of one's own paper, I can envy the coal miner with his bags of free coal and the Covent Garden porter with his cotchell of peas and beans. It seems a pity that neither of these highly paid workers is made to realize by cash-payment the price of the article to which his ever-increasing wage contributes so much.

Why cotchell? I can find no help in lexicography. Did it come from some Irishmen employed in the Garden? Coshery was once a word for a free feast in Ireland or for victuals extorted by chiefs from the humbler members of the clan. Since the Porters' Union now claims to be, and often is, the sovereign of the market, a coshery of vegetables would be a suitable term. Did cotchell come that way?

CYBERNETICS

THE word economics is now widely familiar: it is not so widely known that it originally meant in Greek the law of the house or home, domestic management. When economics had been academically established, a new-comer, Cybernetics, was foisted on to our language. This is another of the upstart words which are, by origin, very old ones. This jargon is spawned by the sciences. So Cybernetics turns up in treatises on Social Science. (I am not greatly impressed by the term Social Science and its jargon. There can be no exact science of Public Affairs, which need general acumen, vigilance and common sense; piling up long words on top is just snow on the roof, professional exhibitionism.) Cybernetics, referred back to Greece and put in plain English, is the art of steering and so of governing.

The Greek for the man at the helm is a word of four syllables, 'Kubernetes'. The Greeks, and especially the Athenians, were maritime people for whom navigation was essential to survival and expansion. They took many of their words and metaphors from the sea. So he who guided the Ship of State was thought of as the Steersman. He was in charge of political navigation. Later on the Romans turned the Greek word 'kubernetes' into 'gubernator', and we have turned that into our Governor. This word Governor has come to mean all sorts of things with us, not only Top Brass but, in slang, father of the family and then any Old Bloke. Governor and Government will not do for the mandarins of the University world, especially in America where long classical words are honey to the intellectuals. So they go back to the Greek word, cut out the Roman form, and dish up a science of Cybernetics. Perhaps it impresses the students of politics, but it does not impress me.

What the ordinary man can remember is that, if he sees Cybernetics in a book or an article or a schedule of lectures, it means the art of governing. Also he can reflect on the curious fact that when the bus-conductor calls him Guv'nor (the bus-conductress probably dubs him Ducks), he is being alluded to as Cox, Helmsman, or Man at the Wheel. The driver who steers the bus is obviously the real exponent of Wheelsmanship — or Cybernetics.

But I have found Cybernetics defined in quite a different way, namely as 'the study of the human brain as compared to electronic computing machines and others which perform certain functions similar to those of the human brain'. Concerning this Eric Partridge writes:

> All this is well worth mentioning, for it may serve to render us not unforgetful of the fact that it was mankind which devised and directed the invention and construction of the electronic brain and its companions; that it is mankind which will steer and guide and control their improvements; that, unless we lose our senses, we shall not allow the instruments to control mankind.

With that sentence I fully agree. We must steer our steersmen.

DEMOGRAPHICAL

MY paper was offering the latest news and views of the situation in a land vexed with bitter conflict. To explain its troubles I was informed that the country suffered from 'demographical pressures'. This left me, despite a classical education, flummoxed. Demos, I was aware, means people and graphe means a drawing or writing. Did the unfortunate region suffer from an excess of popular cartoonists or an overplus of best-selling authors? Resort to the dictionary informed me that demography is that branch of anthropology which is concerned with the statistics of births, deaths and figures of population. So, as far as I could gather, all that was meant by the mention of demographical pressures was the existence of too many natives. I do not see why readers of newspapers should be forced to get up and look for a dictionary in order to comprehend reports written, not for a Congress of Anthropologists, but for a million or more readers not one in a hundred of whom is likely to know exactly what demographical means. A really popular paper, aiming at many more millions, would not, of course, print turgid writing of this kind. It would not only be winning popularity by translating from the Greek into simple English: it would be doing the English language a service. Better English is often written in the papers of vast circulation than in those catering for loftier minds in the various jargons of the sociologist.

DIFFERENTIAL

THE adjective differential has come into frequent use owing to wage-disputes. It is a useful epithet for describing that which differentiates, i.e. causes people or things to differ. The difference between the rewards of skilled and unskilled labour has been reduced lately because the latter is so scarce and therefore there are constant disputes concerning the differential principles and practices involved. But it is our constant habit to turn a fashionable adjective into a fashionable noun. For some reason subordinates are no longer given directions; they receive directives. That is supposed to sound more solemn, important and up to date. In a similar way differential has been turned into a noun and used where the simple difference would once have sufficed. The leading articles in the upper ranges of the Press frequently write about the differentials between differing parties. Before long we shall be reading about 'the consequential of the Government's policy'. To add two syllables is a great pleasure to many.

What an impressive adjective is consequential! It is odd that a consequence or result should have been regarded as being generally a good result and that consequence came to signify weight and value. So a man of consequence became a flattering term and the epithet consequential came to suggest that great one's air of authority and pomp.

I am reminded of a charming advertisement for a certain brand of footwear. We were recommended to purchase 'these courtly and consequential shoes'. They might now be offered to people of consequence as 'these dressy and differential shoes'.

DING-DONG

As an industrious student of gossip I noted that when Miss Diana Dors had taken up residence (no paltry cottage) in Hollywood, she invited the local great ones to a Ding-Dong. A helpful American met my query about ding-dongs by saying that New Yorkers do not entertain with or throw ding-dongs. (Is it not time that we stopped 'throwing' parties as if they were pebbles out to sea or spanners into the works?) Ding-Dong is a Western term which came from the ranches, and usually means a party which, as Damon Runyon would have said, is 'more than somewhat'. This is odd, because one of my dictionaries, after alluding to the repeated sound of bells, said that ding-dong had become an adjective meaning monotonous and tedious. It is surely impossible that any 'do' arranged by Miss Dors could be thus drearily ding-dong. But another dictionary interpretation came to my rescue. There are, after all, ding-dong struggles, and so I read that the adjective ding-dong could also mean 'vigorously maintained, down-right, desperate'. This interpretation seems more applicable to Hollywood ding-dongs.

The eighteenth-century Ding-Dong was called a rout. Those

who were out for a frisk (even Dr Johnson once agreed to join a frisk) looked in at a rout along with other rantipoles, a fine-sounding name of the period for the friskier devotees of the rout. The Soirée and the Conversazione arrived in the following century and were more solemn and sedate, 'An evening social meeting with tea', says one lexicographer of a soirée, and that would not, I fancy, resemble a Hollywood ding-dong. But I think there was more than tea consumed when Sam Weller attended 'a friendly swarry' with the gentlemen's gentlemen at Bath. The menu included 'boiled leg of mutton with the usual trimmings'.

I have also seen a ding-dong described as a shindig. That links up with the old English shindy, which is explained as a variant for shinty. Shinty is not only a Gaelic and vigorous form of what the English call hockey; it is a spree or merry-making and is a lengthening of the word shine. A shine was early nineteenth-century slang for a social gathering, either soberly conversational, as in tea-shine, or more convivial with stronger refreshment available. In my boyhood 'to cut a shine' was to be smart and gay and so to be a likely guest for what is now a shindig or a ding-dong.

The English, and especially the northern English, have retained the single word 'do' for these companionable capers. 'There was quite a do at Mrs Smith's on Saturday.' But this 'do' has a plebeian flavour. Would Hollywood reduce a ding-dong to the less clamorous, less glamorous and less pretentious 'do'?

DISH

ONE often finds that modern slang, American as well as English, contains an old English usage. Accustomed to hearing an attractive young woman described as quite a dish or as a dish with some succulent adjective attached, I was interested to note that in Shakespeare's *Antony and Cleopatra* Enobarbus remarks of his master, when married, for reasons of policy, to the Roman Octavia, that 'he will to his Egyptian dish again'. In *Pericles* the virtuous Marina,

battling against the brothel-keeper, is jeered at as 'a dish of chastity'.
Not all our contemporary dishes could claim to be of that order of
crockery.

DOLORIMETER

AMERICAN medical men have been subjecting pain to an intense
scrutiny and as part of their equipment they have employed an
implement called a dolorimeter.

> O sanguine and subtle Dolores,
> Our lady of Pain!

So Swinburne's rapturous vision of this agonized and agonizing
creature, 'the daughter of Death and Priapus', has been accom-
modated to the prosy arithmetic of a tape-measure. The meter is
sovereign in our world. We know, by gadgetary information, the
heat of our bodies and the speed of our motion on earth and water
and in air. We exactly measure our mileage and our blood-pressure
and now we can do the same for our aches and torments. This may
give the doctor ecstasy: it is no joy to us.

The article in which I read of the Dolorimeter did not explain
how it works; nor did it tell us what accuracy it can achieve. That
is a difficult point, since the writer was most insistent that pain is
largely subjective. You can think yourself into it, as everybody
knows who has begun to worry about tooth or stomach. You can,
if you are a fakir or some monster of iron will, think yourself out of
it, more or less. In any case, we all have our private standards of
suffering: one man's minor ache is another's major agony. How does
a dolorimeter cope with the infinite variety of nervous systems?

I do not know, nor do I greatly care. What I ask of the doctor is
not the reading of his dolorimeter but a swift prescription for a
dolorifuge, if this cumbrous vocabulary is to be kept up. Fortunately the medical science of our time is cunning in device of anaesthetic and analgesic drugs. Swinburne must have been feeling in

fine fettle when he hymned the Lady of Pain with such a glorious mixture of melody and bosh. My note on clap-trap and its application to a painting by Charlotte Brontë might, I now reflect, have included a reference to Swinburne who was indeed a superb minstrel of 'the old malarkey'. I would rather read him, yet again, on Dolores, the splendid and sterile, the subtle and sanguine, with her chapel where virtues are vices, than fuss myself with information about the dolorimeter. Swinburne can help to assuage a toothache or banish a lethargy. The gadget can only turn suffering into sums and convert the misery of the flesh into the misery of mathematics. Give me the drug, poetical or clinical, and let the figures go.

DREAM

D o I want a Dream Home and then to escape from it into a Dream Holiday? These are questions frequently posed by the advertisers in the magazines that I see. Or perhaps the queries are more directly aimed at the Girl Wife who appears so often in the news-columns of the daily and evening Press. It is a strange assumption that all dreams are of perfection. My own, though hardly to be described as nightmares, are usually a crazy, nonsensical jumble of past or quite recent experience. I cannot remember dreaming of a Dream Holiday. More often I seem to be missing trains and boats when making a journey. Frustration-complex? Let the 'psycho' specialists gather round my bedside. Perhaps they or some other medico will kindly order me a Dream Winter in the West Indies on pain of total collapse — with a beneficent employer to pay for it.

Another of these noun-into-adjective favourites is Mercy. If a ship is dispatched with victuals for a storm-bound island or an aeroplane sets out to drop food-parcels on a snow-bound Highland farm, it will certainly be called in the papers a Mercy Ship or Mercy Plane. My well-endowed dispatch to blue lagoons and coral strands, could it miraculously occur, would thus be a Mercy Trip. Such usage of Mercy, or even of the longer Merciful, is absurd since the word means, according to the dictionary, 'forbearance and compassion shown by one person to another who is in his power and has no claim to receive kindness' and then is also employed to signify 'disposition to forgive'. The unfortunate islanders and farmers are not sinners in need of pardon: afflicted by a climatic accident they simply want and merit nourishment and kindly aid. We are not forgiving their trespasses when we send out our Mercy Expeditions: we are merely behaving with normal decency.

But Mercy sounds dramatic and therefore appeals strongly to those incurable romantics, the sub-editors of popular newspapers, the men who have to trim and enhance the news-stories and put up eye-catching and heart-stirring headlines. Mercy Planes and Mercy Ships are far more likely to stir emotion than are mere Food Planes and Aid Ships, just as Dream Holidays are justly supposed to be far more appealing than Holidays which are merely Good. We appear to live in somnolent times. 'And we in dreams behold the Hebrides.' That was sung more than a century ago. Dream Trips now centre rather upon the isle of Capri or upon Blackpool or Clacton for those whose visions of enchantment are less widely vagrant.

Another of the favoured noun-adjectives is Freak. It will be a Freak Storm that has cut off the hungry islanders and crofters and thus launched Mercy Voyages and Flights. It is noticeable that these sub-editorial pets are serviceably short. Brevity is the constant need of the sub-editor. Newspaper columns are narrow and so long words are impossible in headlines. The monosyllable is his dreamwork and nouns usually save a syllable. Hence Freak instead of Freakish. Hence, too, Dream Homes and Dream Holidays. These are properly popular with those who, for a brief caption's sake, have to count the letters of a word, as a miser counts his coins.

Blondes, it may be observed, are always news whereas brunettes are not. That may be due to the famous title of the nineteen-twenties, *Gentlemen Prefer Blondes*, an assertion which may or may not be true, but has certainly become embedded in the public consciousness. On the side of the blonde there is also the fact that she saves the sub-editor a syllable. 'Brunette in Court' may just fail to fit, whereas 'Blonde in Court' can be comfortably squeezed in. Brunettes, if they are in the dock or the witness-box, arrive there without reference to their colour-scheme. Furthermore, though I frequently read of young women (of apparently explosive beauty) described as Blonde Bombshells, I never encounter a Brunette Bombshell. There must surely be some golden girls who could be featured as Red-Head Rockets. But the prize (of publicity) goes always to the fair.

So I expect one day to meet (if only in print) a Dream Blonde on a Freak Flight. Her excursion may be Mercy too, if she is a film-star speeding to the rescue of a producer who suddenly finds himself to be short of 'starlets'.

Leaving the journalistic handling of our sleeping visions we can turn to the loftier vocabulary of the subject. If you seek to be learned in this matter of dreams you can talk of Oneirology. (The Greek word for dream was 'oneiros'.) So the professor called an Oneirologist is an expert on, or interpreter of, dreams. It is a very ancient profession, as students of the Book of Genesis are aware. Joseph's skill in oneirology, or perhaps his natural shrewd-ness, enabled him to explain Pharaoh's dream about the fat and lean kine in terms of years of plenty and years of famine. This got Joseph out of prison and into fine linen and high office; it also promoted him to an exalted tenancy of the second of the royal chariots.

Meanwhile the psychoanalysing oneirologists of our time are not much concerned with dreams as visions of the ideal; nightmares are better matter for them. No Dream Homes or Dream Holidays are the result of their research. Instead, they find the most appalling deposits in our emotional interiors when they start to interpret our nocturnal fantasies. It was well said of these oneirological diggers and delvers that 'they go down deeper and come up dirtier than any other form of underground worker'.

ECTOMORPH

THE athlete used to develop his muscles: now he does more; he swells out his vocabulary. When I was a small boy it was the right thing to have a Sandow Outfit complete with dumb-bells. Later on, the dumb-bell went completely out of fashion: instead of gripping and brandishing artificial weights the youngster was made to do more natural exercises: the physical jerk superseded the weighted bars and 'bells'. Dumb-bell later became slang for a *dumm* creature, a nit-wit.

Now the acquisition of physical fitness has become a branch of science as well as an organized procedure of the Welfare State. Of course, as a science, it possesses the appropriate jargon. We have a Central Council of Physical Recreation and one of its learned authorities has divided us, for purposes of advice and treatment, into Ectomorphs, Endomorphs and Mesomorphs. Since the Greek word 'ektos' means outside and 'morphe' means shape or figure, one might expect an ectomorph to be a vast fellow who needs an outsize when he buys his vests and pants. Not at all: he is a thin, frail, grey-hound type, nimble, and with a good expectation of life. He is deemed to be unsuited for sports with violent physical contacts. In other words, let him avoid boxing and wrestling. If not, some other 'morph' will flatten him out.

The Greek word 'endon' means within, yet, mysteriously, the endomorph, likely to 'put the kibosh' on the fragile ectomorph, is fat, ponderous and best suited with a bowling-green or a fishing-rod. (It is new information to me that angling and adiposity go together.) It is all very mysterious. Why is a within-shaped man, as the word endomorph implies, regarded as clumsy and obese?

The mesomorph is thickset, a healthy gorilla-type, who enjoys his exercise and must stick to it if he is not to sink into fatty de-generacy. This word is not so baffling. The Greek 'meson' means the middle, and so the mesomorph stands half way between the skinny ectomorph and the fleshy endomorph and could presumably knock out the former and puncture the latter. What is gained, we may reasonably wonder, by piling up adjectives of this kind? The vocabulary of the new athleticism is itself ponderous and puffy, in short, endomorphic.

EMPIRICAL AND ESCHEW

EMPIRICAL is a word which one may meet in the loftier kind of publications, whose authors call suspect policies empirical. I remember Neville Cardus in his cricket reports describing a batsman's stroke as 'purely empirical'.

Empirical has nothing to do with Empire, although it looks as though it came from the same root. Empire really should be Impire and Emperor Imperor, since they come from the Latin Imperium and Imperator which mean rule and ruler. It is strange that we should have kept the adjective Imperial with the right vowel, and flattened the 'i' into 'e' in the case of the nouns, Empire and Emperor.

Empiric and Empirical are derived from the Greek language, in which 'peira' means trial. The empirical man was one who tested everything and reached his conclusion through experience. That is to say, he formed his principles on the basis of his observed facts, which seems to be a very sensible proceeding. But there is another philosophy which starts by asserting a principle and then maintains that the observed facts are only intelligible in the light of this principle. Thus the religious empiricist says that things seen and felt around us prove the existence of God. His opponent assumes the existence of God and says that things seen and felt are only intelligible on that assumption.

During the course of time the latter party, who are contemptuous of knowledge based on trial and experience, have managed to give a nasty twist to the adjective empirical, so that it came to imply quackery or charlatanism. Hence the politician's sneer at his rival's 'empirical policies' and Cardus's implication that an empirical stroke is one made by a batsman deserting the principles of the game.

To my mind, empirical should be an adjective of highest praise. Surely the best results are got by the old, proverbial means to success, 'Try, try again'.

I would link eschew with empirical because both figure in the same species of prose style. For example, I notice in a leading article in my morning's paper that the Government is wisely eschewing a certain policy. I almost expected the writer to announce that it behoved the Government to eschew, etc. etc. Why this antiquated English? Does it add to gravity in counsel, does it make friends and gain influence? In no other section of the paper would you meet eschewal or eschuance (both nouns used to exist). If a reporter wrote that, on inquiry, he found the people of a certain town to be eschewing the arrival of still more trippers he would have his copy severely sub-edited. Even a literary or dramatic critic who wrote that Mr So-and-So has on this occasion eschewed his usual taste for violence would be deemed somewhat pompous. But the sages of the centre page can keep up their behoves and eschews as if they were writing with quills and by candlelight in a Fleet Street earlier than that of George Augustus Sala.

Eschew, from Old French Eschiver or Escheuer, means no more than avoid or shun. I fancied that it was a favourite with the translators of the Authorized Version of the Bible, but, on referring to Cruden, I found that it occurs only twice, once in each of the Testaments. On both occasions it is 'evil' that is to be eschewed. Shakespeare has it only once:

> What cannot be eschewed must be embraced.

The sight of Eschew makes me want to laugh. The discreet avoidance which it implies becomes confused, by the sound of the word, with spitting out a chewed mouthful. But it remains a pet of preachers in pulpit or at the desk. I was once so constant a writer of leading articles that I would be the last to mock a profession whose members, toiling to instruct the world in how to conduct its affairs, are obviously confronted with a tall order. As a mere youngster, there was I, commanded to tell expert and experienced people how to manage their businesses and frame their policies on all sorts of subjects. The basic supposition of a leader column is the omniscience of the journalist who can put everybody right on every topic. I never deemed myself all-wise, but I had to put up some show of all-round profundity in order to earn my keep. Absurd as was this performance, I can fairly claim that I never warned the members of the Government that it behoved them to eschew, etc. etc.

GANNET

OUR use of birds in simile and metaphor has its curious aspects. We pay a generous avian compliment on the golf-course, since the player who does a hole in one stroke less than the scratch figure allotted, e.g. by holding a scheduled 'five' in four shots, is said to have got a 'Birdie'. Should he achieve the rare feat of doing a 'five' in three strokes, he has accomplished an Eagle. On the other side of the picture, we treat owls with contempt. There is a paradox here. The owl was the companion bird of Athene, goddess of wisdom, and so an early symbol of sagacity. Yet we now employ the adjective owlish to describe a dull or silly fellow. Owls, I fancy, are neither particularly clever nor particularly crass; but the ancients paid them the tribute due to high intelligence while we demean them as dolts.

The same is true of gulls who show some cunning, at least in the concealment of their eggs laid on the sandy or pebbly shore. But gull was early made the name for a simpleton, while the verb to gull means the process of cozening a fool. The apparent felicity of the soaring, singing lark has also been belittled. Our 'larking about' suggests a roughness of humour and not an ecstasy of animation. But ducks, and even hens in Scotland, have been regarded as proper terms for essentially lovable people, with geese regarded only as witless.

Naturally the predatory, raptorial birds have been much called on for a metaphor. We salute the eagle, and not only on the golf-course, as shown in the Book of Proverbs and the fiction of Ethel M. Dell.

> There be three things which are too wonderful for me: yea, four which I know not.
> The way of an eagle in the air: the way of a serpent upon a rock: the way of a ship in the midst of the sea: and the way of a man with a maid.

The author of the Biblical Proverbs overlooked the way of a maid with a man, which can sometimes be more miraculous than its converse. But few will dispute his tribute to the aquiline monarch of the mountain skies.

We are, on the other hand, unkind to hawks whose keen-eyed flights, or hoverings and swoops, in pursuit of their natural way of life should not be associated with especial cruelty or greed. But to call a man a hawk is not to flatter his professional or financial activities.

That brings me at last to the gannet. A friend sent me a remarkable phrase used by an airman, who, while confessing his ignorance on the subject of English literature, added, 'But I'm a gannet for gen'. (Gen, of course, meant information to him.) Anybody who has seen off the coast that powerful bird, the gannet or Solan goose, poised over the sea and then swooping with one straight tremendous dive to catch a coveted fish will appreciate the vigour of the metaphor. No student in the world could more voraciously pursue knowledge than one who could be called 'a gannet for gen'. Being myself a gannet for words, I am entranced by this wonderful description of an avid pursuit.

GERONTOLOGY

GERONTOLOGISTS abound. In 1957 they were pleasantly assembled among the Italian Lakes, advising each other and ourselves on the technique of living longer and achieving a larger 'geras', which is the Greek for old age. If they had a proper respect for shrines they would go to Israel for their next concourse, as the Moham-medan goes to Mecca or the Shakespearian to Stratford. For thereabouts lived their chief examplar: there should Methuselah be honoured by the sages of senectitude, which is the Latin for Gerontology. Incidentally, I note that the *Oxford English Dictionary* prefers geratology to gerontology, the science of old age, not the science of old men. The 'g' it seems should be soft and the 'e' long. So now, if you are a Methuselist, you have the 'gen'.

Bernard Shaw wrote his famous Pentateuch *Back to Methuselah* as a summons to endurance. Young men, he thought, have no experience: only age brings wisdom, and so the longer our rulers live, the wiser will our rulers be. He did not prevail, and it is still commonly held that sixty or, at the latest, seventy is the proper age for retirement from the governance of the nation or the direction of business. Shaw cried out for a Gerontocracy, a government of old men, and did so with such emphasis that a centenarian was a child in his eyes. What we needed, in his opinion, to achieve perfection of regimen was an Oligarchy of Ancients, obstinately enduring for centuries on the Methuselist model.

But the Paradise of the Arch-veterans which he drew was of such a bloodless and an abstract kind, a vortex of purely intellectual activity, that playgoers, being average sensual men and women, were not favourably impressed by his lengthily advocated heaven.

Returning to the medical Senectudinarians, I find that Harley Street is in its usual state of self-contradiction. On the one hand, a stay-at-home authority insists, to the great relief of smokers, that cancer is caused by worry and not by the lethal constituents of the cigarette. So we can best defeat that scourge by keeping calm and cheerful. On the other hand, I find that our professors of geron-tology, conferring in Italy, say exactly the opposite. 'The doctors from 26 countries', I read, 'all seem agreed that the most fatal thing you can do in later life is to hanker after a restful retirement and peace of mind.' One insisted that 'peace of mind is for the birds and not for human beings'. We must sweat, strive and fret in order to score a happy hundred. No cease, no calm, no cottage in the country. Work and worry are the props of the geratophile.

That cuts out the consumption of tranquillizing drugs and completely contradicts the notion that illness, including cancer as well as ulcers, comes with stress. I naturally wonder whether it is worth while paying attention (and large fees and salaries) to a profession so rich in contradictory counsel. Are we to become Methuselists by sitting back or by jumping to it? Are work and worry life-givers or life-takers? When doctors so violently disagree, why worry about what they say?

GIMMICK

WORDS easily become vogue-words. When somebody creates or imports a novelty, we all pounce on it together. One is felt to be in the swim if one can garnish a paragraph with this new-comer. Not long ago it became impossible to read a notice of a film or a play in which the word gimmick did not appear. It has passed from the players to the politicians. When Mr Macmillan became Prime Minister one political correspondent assured us that the new Premier had no gimmick. In my English innocence I had to delve about to find what it meant and how it arrived.

As I surmised from the way in which it was so busily employed, it generally means a trick or dodge. American writers discuss gimmicks in politics, meaning tactical devices. More often, the word is used to signify a writer's or an actor's routine device for getting effects. Alliteration was the gimmick of Swinburne when he wrote about 'the lilies and languors of virtue' and 'the roses and raptures of vice'. Many comedians have their gimmicks, either as catchphrase, theme-song, or bit of 'business', which they exploit in most of their appearances. I remember an old music-hall comedian called Phil Ray who began his turn by announcing, 'I always abbrieve.

It's a hab.' Never to finish a word was his (not wildly diverting) gimmick.

It is a queer-looking word. Apparently it is a slang version of gimcrack. The latter was first used of a craftsman's inlaid work, but, because such work might be feeble and fanciful, gimcrack came to suggest the useless, the merely showy, the trumpery article. From that followed the employment of gimcrack to describe a poor kind of artifice and a shallow device. So the habitual dodges of the entertainer, who had discovered a ruse that was sure of a laugh, became his gimcrack or his gimmick.

The word jim-jam appears to have been another corruption of gimcrack and meant a knick-knack or trifle. But, for some inexplicable reason, it then became associated with delirium tremens. So to get an attack of 'the horrors' was described in slang as 'getting the jim-jams'. Jim-jam, thus used, is a queer cousin of gimmick. But some comedians' repeated gimmicks do become so tiresome that they may arouse in us something akin to jim-jammery.

GRAPE-VINE

'I HEARD it on the grape-vine.' 'The City grape-vine talks of a quick rise in Tankos.' This now popular tree is a fairly recent growth in my own experience. In meaning, it is roughly equivalent to Bush Telegraph: and as a telegraph it seems to have begun its life nearly a century ago. My *Dictionary of Americanisms on Historical Principles* tells me that 'grape-vine telegraph' means 'any surreptitious means of transmitting information, allegedly first used of a telegraph line constructed in 1859 between Placerville and Virginia City'. The American Civil War naturally encouraged grape-vine communication and the term later became associated with insubstantial and fabricated news. It was then said of one General that 'he is no sensationalist: he is not given to grape-vine dispatches'. The grape-vine, with its tendentious tendrils, has continued to flourish as a typical growth in the swamps of rumour.

Rumour was originally 'voice or sound', but came to signify either a general din or, more commonly, a report eagerly disseminated and not to be believed. To Shakespeare rumour was 'a pipe, blown by surmises, jealousies, conjectures' and an instrument so simple that 'the blunt monster, with uncounted heads', the wavering multitude, could easily play upon it. To Carlyle it was 'the distillation of history'. It is hard to understand why we have adopted the American grape-vine for what was once called 'the bruit of the town'. This cultivation of the word vine can perhaps be justified by the heady liquor of news that is often pressed from its too communicative grapes. The City grape-vine has been known to lead the too credulous investor far up the vineyard.

GUBBINSES

ONE of the chief personal objectives during the early months of 1957 was the procuring of more miles from each gallon of strictly rationed petrol. Various implements and contrivances were suggested for coping with this problem. Concerning these Mr Courtenay Edwards, the motoring expert of the *Daily Mail*, recently reported some comments. Here is one example.

> Said Mr Peter Mays of Dorking: 'Engine designers are not complete clots and they have had years to perfect carburettor design. They don't always design for maximum power or maximum economy. Often they go for jolly good compromise as represented by the average family saloon.'
> Mr Mays summed up: 'Take it from me you can save more petrol by how you drive than with the gubbinses now floating around.'

This use of gubbinses for gadgets or ingenuities may be old: it is unusual today and it struck me as an interesting revival. There is presumably a singular form, 'a gubbins'.

Most lexicographers are unhelpful in the matter of gubbins.

But *Chambers's Dictionary* has some notions which lead us far from the petrol-pump and up-to-date gadgetry. We are there reminded that the Gubbins were a half-savage race in Devonshire described by the pastoral poet William Browne and by Fuller in his *Worthies*. Except for Dartmoor's occasional escaped convicts there are luckily no more 'gubbinses now floating round' — at least not of this wild Western type.

GUTS

'HE's got guts.' Ought this to appear nowadays in written English when the writer is avoiding coarseness and slang? Why not? I owe to Mr Frank Whitaker, the editor of *Country Life*, the reminder that the better accepted word for guts, pluck, was once no less intestinal. Pluck was an old word for the 'heart, liver, lungs, and sometimes other viscera', presumably because such things were plucked out of the bodies of animals by carnivorous man, either to be separated and retained as edible offal or thrown away. Dean Swift used pluck for heart. It 'vexed him to the pluck' that he was prevented from walking out on a fine day. So, with the entrails forgotten, from the stout heart came the transition and promotion of pluck to signify high courage. Unfortunately for guts the word has an ugly look. None the less, since it shares its rise from bowels to bravery with the now respectable pluck, it has a justified existence in a serious writer's proper vocabulary.

HAGGIS

SOMETHING new about haggis — the fact that it derives from Middle English. This will hardly worry Scots who may well be weary of the English notion that they go (or would gladly go) through life consuming nothing but the native broth, haggis and whisky. No depreciation of those articles is intended. But all nations are entitled to resent labels unnecessarily applied. Haggis has become, in English fancy, the Scots' gimmick, if that word must be used; consequently it will only make Scots smile when they are informed by their own *Scottish National Dictionary* that haggis comes from a Middle English verb meaning to cut or chop, and that the Northern English, and possibly the Southern too, were hagging their meat at table (and possibly each other too in their incessant baronial wars) some eighty years before the Scots hagged up most of a sheep (except the mutton) and sewed it with spice and oatmeal in its paunchy container.

The English idea that the Scots regard haggis as a peculiar delicacy is absurd. The Laird took the mutton and left the hagged remains to the fireside ingenuity of the shepherd's wife. The result is not at all bad and may indeed justify some of the Burnsian gusto. 'Great chieftain o' the puddin' race!' No doubt. But there are other and better things than puddins.

HERMETICALLY

'THE rooms are hermetically sealed.' One is constantly hearing of this hermetical insulation and protection against draughts. Nowadays, sealing seems inadequate or even unthinkable without this obscure adverb. But how many know exactly what they mean when they talk of closing and fastening with hermetical thoroughness?

They might, in fact, say, more simply, 'magically sealed'. If we trace the ancestry of the word hermetic to its source we are taken back to ancient Egypt. The Pharaohs had, among their many gods, a deity of science and alchemy who was called Thoth. The Greeks, who derived so much from Egypt, awarded the attributes of Thoth to their own god Hermes, whom the Romans later called Mercury. Hermes was known as 'Trismegistos', thrice-powerful. Among other things, he was the controller of all chemical magic. To seal a thing up completely was regarded by early societies and even in the Middle Ages as immensely difficult: it needed the art of Hermes, the hermetical touch, the wizardry of the alchemist. So when glass vessels were closed completely by melting some of the glass and letting it stiffen over the opening, this was called hermetical sealing. And now we hardly ever make anything really tight without going back to the old gods of Egypt and Greece and paying our unconscious tribute to the magic of Thoth and Hermes.

Hermes also gave us Hermaphrodite to signify a plant, animal or person in which or in whom both kinds of sexual characteristics are united. Hermes had a son by Aphrodite (the Roman Venus), who was so much loved by a water-nymph that she asked the gods to unite them. When this odd request was granted to the full, the couple became one body, half-male, half-female, a fate both unkind and unearned; Kipling jestingly called the Royal Marine or Jolly 'a giddy harumphrodite, soldier an' sailor too'. Among his other achievements, Hermes has been, by accident, a great word-maker.

HICCOUGH

LENGTHENING words is a current form of intellectual pretension; spelling, too, can be affected by the same sense of superiority. I was amused to discover from my dictionary that hiccough is just a mistake; but it is a snobbish, not a vulgar, error. Someone apparently thought that hiccuping looked rather plebeian and, assuming a cough to be a part of this embarrassing activity, pedantically spelled it hiccoughing. Hiccup, if you want to know its unpleasant constituents, is 'an involuntary spasm of the respiratory organs consisting in a quick inspiratory movement of the diaphragm checked suddenly by the closure of the glottis', the glottis being the upper part of the windpipe. More popularly put, a hiccup is an 'oops-deary' and it is worth noting that upsy or oopsy was used in an old word for toping. Drinking 'Upsy-Dutch' was the deep draught of the malt-worm (lovely word!) and also a compliment to the valiant potations of the 'swag-bellied Hollander' as Shakespeare called him. Swilling in 'Upsy-Dutch' manner was also, presumably, a hiccup-maker.

Next to hiccup in my dictionary I noticed 'Hic Jacet', two Latin words meaning 'here lies'. They were turned into an English phrase, owing to their frequent sepulchral appearances, by Tennyson, who wrote of 'the cold *hic jacets* of the dead'. I mention this because, in setting a competition for a literary review, I once asked for 'An Epitaph on a Good Thirst killed by Kindness'. I gave the prize to the brief and brilliant reply:

'Hic(!) Jacet.'

In this connection I was pleased to discover from an *Encyclopaedia of Beer*, published by the literary as well as liquorish House of Whitbread, that ale was brewed in Egypt about 2000 B.C. The Egyptian name for it was Hequp, which could hardly be better. It establishes the hiccup, at least by its sound, among the earliest absorptions of thirsty man and suggests that the Pharaohs, if they considered ale a sufficiently regal drink, may have endured 'involuntary spasms of the respiratory organs' after downing a pint and named the liquor according to its consequences.

LOLLY

No slang alters more rapidly than that describing the pleasures of life, especially money and intoxication. As to the latter, I heard it said of an elderly actress that she maintained the lingo of her period. 'She talks about being blotto.' I do not know what will be in vogue by the time this note is printed. Presumably plastered and stinking will have become 'period', as blotto has been for a generation.

In the matter of money we have discarded a lot of old favourites. Would a schoolboy of today know what 'oof' meant? That word could now be classified as 'Early P. G. Wodehouse'. The contemporary 'lovely' who gets a big film contract is usually described in the papers most concerned with these promotions as being 'in the lolly'. Lolly is, presumably, a shortened form of lollipop, a veteran term for a boiled sweet. This makes 'plenty of lolly' an equivalent to the 'sugar' which Damon Runyon's Broadway characters were always striving (or failing) to acquire. Another piece of Runyonese for money was potatoes. It is possible to make alcohol out of potatoes, as out of many other unlikely articles, but the potato, when past its childhood, and boiled in its maturity, is to me a singularly dull tuber and therefore very oddly accepted as a term for gold. The lolly sucked by an urchin on the end of a stick is itself far from romantic and does not seem, at first sight, to merit a place in the glittering world of Midas. But at least it has its own succulence and is a better alternative to the vanished oof, rhino, dibs, spondulicks and all the queer money-tokens of the past than is the earthy, starchy potato. Surely the fortunate would rather be 'in the lolly' than 'in the spuds'.

MALADJUSTED

ADJUST, and adjustment, and maladjusted are words very happily adjusted to our fashion of polite evasion. They sound so reasonable. They accommodate contraries, either personal or theoretical. They make smooth any harsh surface: they remove the blot from ugliness; they ease the severity of condemnation; they mitigate the grimness of words like sin and sinner. Hence the favour shown, in a compassionate society, to 'maladjusted juvenile delinquents'. But these pests may be ungovernable young thugs. Yet nobody must dare to suggest that such nuisances could make themselves otherwise by an effort of will and by realizing that they are responsible for their conduct. Was there ever a time with more talk of freedom for nations and individuals — and with less belief in free will?

When people excuse their own faults by blaming their parents, their childhood and their social or economic condition they are making a natural evasion. What is remarkable is the modern taste for exculpating others (and often very nasty others) by explaining that, if they did knock a defenceless old woman on the head and rifle her till, it was really no fault of the assailants. Heredity had been unkind to them and their upbringing had been unfortunate.

E

How could they be responsible for their vile actions, since they were thus maladjusted? Of course there are some unlucky youngsters whose adjustment, if we must use the word, has been deficient through no fault of their own. I would not be hard on all such explanations. But the plea of social misfortune is made so often that I am now very suspicious when those accused of some filthy callousness or brutality are defended with this plea of maladjustment. It is time for plainer speaking.

Adjustment has become so fashionable in our talk that it finds its way into the popular magazines and their advertising columns. Consider the contemporary counsel, now so frequent, given to the multitude of those who would be thinner. There is no use of the brief words, fat and slim. The new technique soars above monosyllables. The obese or adipose are instructed in how to slenderize. Previously, in descriptions of the path to slenderization, they would have been told to diet or bant. (Bant is a back-formation from Banting, which was the family name of an early advocate of cutting down the poundage by cutting out the starch.) Now it is tactfully and suavely suggested that the slenderizing parties practise 'menu-adjustment'. After that, presumably, if the menus be rigorously reformed, they can practise waistline adjustment of their clothing. Writing as one who has gloomily to consider his diet, I prefer the old banting and dieting to the new reformation of my maladjusted menus.

Inevitably adjustment, being now a vogue-word, has found its way into art-criticism. An Exhibition of 'British Abstract Art' in 1956, shown at the Institute of Contemporary Art, was called Statements, because the artists not only showed their work but expounded their artistic creed in the catalogue. Mr John Forrester put forward his point of view thus:

> The direction for creative endeavour is clearly marked by the human history of achievement and failure. This direction leads to a social form which contains a developable theme of cohesive community and individual conscious awareness. The

possibilities of attaining this desired state are made arduous by the constantly rising barriers which are manifest in the superficial level of authoritative directory, the arbiter of which is destructive indoctrination to an apparent optimal existence of adjustment, the adjustment at all times being regulated complementary to the source of direction. Undoubtedly this state constitutes the greatest dissipation of the immense constructive potential to be found in correlated social awareness; national insularity which is thus bred becomes oppression for the individual upon whom the complete social structure evolves.

This declaration of creed and explanation of paintings admittedly not simple of purpose did not leave me much wiser. Perhaps my stupidity is to blame. I confess that I am maladjusted to this level of exposition.

MATRICULATE

THE matricula is the list of persons belonging to an order or society. Hence an admitted student matriculates at a University. The word is a queer child of matrix, the womb. From its physical significance matrix derived further meanings as a place of origin or source of growth. So a society or University may be said to grow or develop from its number of matriculated members. Heraldry retains the term among its many verbal treasures. I read that, by pleasure of the Lord Lyon King of Arms:

the Ensigns armorial of Shaw of Tordarroch are being matriculated in the Public Register of all Arms and Bearings in Scotland in the name of Charles John Shaw of Tordarroch, 16th Hereditary Head or Chief of the Clan of Ay of Tordarroch within the Clan Mackintosh and in cadency from the Arms of the Chief of Clan Mackintosh conform to his Lordship's Interlocutor and Warrant to the Lyon Clerk for that effect of date July 6, 1957.

Cadence or Cadency, the state of a cadet, means the descent of a younger branch from the main line of a family as well as 'the flow of verses or periods'.

Heraldry writes cadently of its cadets when it is accepting its matriculations. As one who is not horrified by split infinitives I note with interest that the Lord Lyon King of Arms states that he is 'pleased to officially recognize' this matter of the Chief of Ay's matriculated Arms and Bearings.

MEWS

WE continually read of Mews Flats. These, as a rule, are transmogrified upper parts of old urban stables now used as garages. (It may surprise the reader to know that transmogrified is not slang, but a well-established dictionary word and as old as Oliver Cromwell.) To occupy a central London mews flat may be quite costly and modish: in the hay-loft, where once the coachman laid his drowsy head, a film-starlet may now be giving the kind of party which is called a ding-dong.

It is a fair bet that the lady in the mews does not know why her address carried this name. It goes back to the dropping, not of a hat, but of a feather. To mew was to moult. (It was a form of the verbal root that gives us mutable and mutation.) The hawks kept by men of fashion for their sport had to be penned up while they were shedding their plumage, that is to say moulting or mewing. This form of caging-in took over the name of that changing process and was called mewing too. Thus mewing became, in Elizabethan times, a general name for incarceration. Those who were put through *A Midsummer Night's Dream* in their school-days may remember the sentence pronounced on the rebellious Hermia. If she did not marry as ordered, she had this dim future:

> For aye to be in shady cloister mew'd
> And live a barren sister all your life.

The royal hawks, when mewing, were mewed up at Charing Cross.

Then, when hawking became less fashionable, the mewing-place was turned into the royal stables. So the Charing Cross Stables were called the Mews. Later the word Mews was applied to all stables: later still, stables were often changed into garages. The garages themselves became mews. There might well be a singular mew, but I have never met it. Mews, thus spelled, looks rather a mean word, suggesting the stray cat. As a matter of fact it is highly aristocratic, since our starlet in her mews flat draws her address from one of the several sports of ancient kings.

The use of Mews in what is called a purlieu of elegance (see note on Purlieu later) is an old one. Here is a passage from *Little Dorrit* which shows that the Mews Street of mid-Victorian London had much resemblance to the same haunts today.

Mews Street, Grosvenor Square, was not absolutely Grosvenor Square itself, but it was very near it. It was a hideous little street of dead wall, stables, and dunghills, with lofts over coach-houses inhabited by coachmen's families, who had a passion for drying clothes, and decorating their window-sills with miniature turnpike gates. The principal chimney-sweep of that fashionable quarter lived at the blind end of Mews Street; and the same corner contained an establishment much frequented about early morning and twilight, for the purchase of wine-bottles and kitchen-stuff. Punch's shows used to lean against the dead wall in Mews Street, while their proprietors were dining elsewhere; and the dogs of the neighbourhood made appointments to meet in the same locality. Yet there were two or three small airless houses at the entrance end of Mews Street, which went at enormous rents on account of their being abject hangers-on to a fashionable situation; and whenever one of these fearful little coops was to be let (which seldom happened, for they were in great request), the house agent advertised it as a gentlemanly residence in the most aristocratic part of town, inhabited solely by the élite of the beau monde.

One of the all-powerful Barnacle family lived in such a 'Mew'.

MODEL

MODEL is one of our current vogue-words. Countless young women of pleasing aspect are now described as models. When a bright girl gets into 'the news' and is asked about her ambitions, she usually says that she wants to be a 'model' or to do modelling. The model who posed for an artist is as old as the seventeenth century, but the New Model Regiment of Women includes mannequins — this word seems to be losing favour — and all who are photographed for beauty's sake in the display of fashions in advertisements or on the covers of illustrated papers.

The dictionary gives model, as verb, noun and adjective, a remarkable number of meanings. The verb includes among its interpretations to produce in clay, to give shape to anything, to organize, to imitate, or to make a tool of. The adjective is highly complimentary, implying that we needs must love the highest when we see it and that we imitate only the best. Hence model conduct. The noun covers summary, epitome, mould and miniature as well as an ideal.

That all the girls of today setting out to be models understand the full implication of the chosen title is doubtful. It sometimes appears from the news reports of personal and social events and complications that an aspirant to a model career may be what is now commonly called 'a crazy mixed-up kid'. In other words, a muddled model.

MONOPOLY

IN a communication concerning Holidays Abroad For Boys, a communication coming from a school which I believe to be a good one, I was astonished to discover that one seaside resort is recommended as having 'a monopoly of European sunshine'. Was this absurd remark put on paper by a schoolmaster?

Monopoly has become a vogue-word because it has been a

subject of public inquiry with legislation presumed to follow. Once it meant what the name, Greek for sole-selling, implies. One person or body was granted by the Crown the sole right to trade in certain articles. Now these officially granted privileges have been replaced by trading groups whose members unite to fix and maintain selling prices and are able to enforce these prices by threatening to deny supplies of popular goods to retailers who seek to increase their turnover by cutting prices and attracting more customers.

I need not go into the ethics of this procedure, which are not always as bad as they seem. Booksellers, for example, need their net price agreement with the publishers in order to prevent the competition of stores which are not book-shops, take none of the booksellers' stocking risks, and seek only to cash in on a few very popular books by cutting the price and collecting customers. These book sales need not be economic since it is hoped that the purchasers of a 'best seller' at a discount will also be attracted by the exhibits in the food and clothing departments and spend accordingly.

Such competition is unfair to the ordinary booksellers whose attempts to maintain the published price, until such time as 're-maindering' is permitted, can be described as monopolistic, but are, in fact, reasonable considering the difficulty of selling books at all. Monopoly is much discussed: it is also much played as a species of parlour-game which must horrify Socialists by encouraging the public to gamble in site-values. So Monopoly has become one of the fashionable words which are flung about loosely and far and wide. 'A monopoly of European sunshine' is an example of this laxity. Presumably the writer meant to say that the resort in question held a European sunshine record, a statement which must be hard to justify. What, in fact, he did imply was that that place had bought up all the available European sunshine and was selling it at its own price.

Once a word has become fashionable people, even well-educated people, will drag it in continually with little concern for meaning. (See later note on Overall.) The use of Streamlined is another example of this habit. Because it effectively described an effective kind of mechanical design, it has been scattered about as an adjective of approbation for almost any kind of economical service. Policies and plans are streamlined: accounts and balance sheets are streamlined: brighter cricket is called streamlined cricket. I should not be surprised to learn that the seaside resort with the sunshine monopoly has streamlined catering in streamlined hotels.

MORON

'NOTHING will be tolerated which does not pander to the lowest common denominator of moronicism.' That is a mouthful, or more properly, a nibful, from an indignant letter to an editor. An arithmetical denominator, as the Lower School knows, is 'the number given below the line in a vulgar fraction, which gives the denomination or value of the parts into which the integer is divided'. But I do not think that the angry correspondent meant more by his L.C.D. of moronicism than a depth of folly.

Moron is now a common term for a fool, ignoramus, or victim of 'arrested intellectual development'. It is the neuter of the Greek adjective for foolish and therefore, meaning a stupid thing, rudely denies humanity to the 'clot' in question. It is an American import, whose arrival in Britain is dated at 1913. It has not become widely popular and large numbers of the population would not know what was meant if they were nominated moronic. But moron has the advantage of its ponderous sound: it well describes a lumpish, not a flighty, fool. Moronic and moronism can pass. But why moronicism? The explanation can only be that an extra syllable always appeals to those who wish to thump their fellows with the cudgel of prolixity.

MUSHROOMING

I NOTE in my *Daily Mail* that round Lourdes, owing to increasing faith in miraculous cures, picture-postcards are having record sales and hotels are briskly mushrooming. To mushroom is now a verb in fairly common use for any speed of upstart growth. Quantity is also implied. I approve of mushrooming: to write thus is less laborious for the reader as well as for the author than to be told of hotels that spring up in numbers almost overnight. Let us, for imagery, cherish our vegetable growths. I see no harm in asserting that among the young men of my suburb who aspire to intellectual or artistic status beards have fungused lately.

Mushrooming preserves the old tradition of popular journalism that every effort must be made to avoid the ordinary and obvious word. When in boyhood I used to write games reports for the school magazine, I drew on the daily Press for my descriptive style. It was then a point of honour with sporting journalists never to call a thing by its ordinary name. The goal-posts were always the uprights. The ball was the leather or the sphere. The weather was laid on by Old Sol or Jupiter Pluvius. To this mode I conformed and, if mushrooming had then been in vogue, I would have written that while Binks was plying the willow his score mushroomed. There were in my vocabulary, which admittedly owed much to the masters of Press-Box English, no such things as wickets or balls that kept low. Would I have written 'Binks was then bowled, having missed a ball which kept low'? Nothing so flat could come from one of my apprenticeship. Say rather, 'Binks failed to connect with a daisy-cutter which shattered his timber-yard'.

The flight from the ordinary now persists in political rather more than in sporting journalism. Nothing, for example, is nowadays merely caused, started, or begun. It is sparked off or, more briefly, sparked: then it flares: or else it is triggered off. One has to imagine our public men as brisk dealers in arson or gunnery. These terms have been kept very busy lately and I have seen one of the most dignified of our morning papers announce in its leading article that a certain incident had triggered off a debate in the House of Commons. Eloquence, no doubt, mushroomed accordingly.

'Sparked off' is now so frequent that no industrial dispute can be permitted to start without this suggestion of a flash in the factory.

Where there is natural tinder for sparks to kindle, this does well enough. But it is surprising to read in the journalism of the Left that the folly of the employers has sparked off a deluge of strikes.

NARCISSIST

THOSE who have missed (or escaped) a classical education need a dictionary of antiquities if they are to understand the jargon of modern psychology. Narcissism, for example, is a word in use in those quarters. One occasionally reads of types called Narcissist and to many the term must be puzzling. What is thus labelled is the habit of self-admiration, and the word is derived from a young man and not from a flower. The bud was named after the boy, not the boy after the bud. The story of this youth also explains our use of the word Echo.

Narcissus, in the Greek legend, was untouched by love. A young woman who had got into the bad books of Hera, the jealous and angry Queen of the Gods, was punished by being turned into Echo; she thus became a creature with no control over her tongue. She could neither speak before others spoke nor keep quiet after others had spoken. This unhappy nymph, doomed to eternal repetition, was obviously a public nuisance, and one can hardly blame Narcissus for remaining wearily aloof when she fell madly in love with him. Echo, thus rebuffed, pined and died of grief and then it was the opinion of the gods that Narcissus had committed the sins of pride and cruelty. So he had to be punished for his treatment of the girl. He was compelled to fall in love with his own image seen in a pool of water. As he could do nothing but stare at himself thus mirrored, he too pined away and was changed into the flower that bears his name. The Greek gods, far from frigid themselves, had no mercy for this unresponsive as well as self-centred youth.

Hence the Narcissist of today is a person gripped by inordinate self-love and egotistic vanity. Surely the luckless Narcissus has been hardly treated for not yielding to the noisy and monotonous lady called Echo: would any of the punitive deities who condemned him have put up with her for long? Echo, incidentally, is a name well based on the sound that it describes. Shout into a quarry or against walls and E-cho does suggest the noise that will return.

Sociologists like to employ the turgid lingo of the psychologists. I noticed that an American writer about racial matters describes the white man's preference for exclusively white company as 'Group-Narcissism'.

NAVVY

THE use of the word 'navvy' for a toiler, principally with the spade, is, I suppose, growing rare. As I remarked when discussing bum-marees, workers of all kinds are very shy of what they think to be nicknames and regard them as 'obnoxious'. Navvy may be deemed a nickname and so General Labourer is preferred. But the name of Navvy has a history and might well be a word of pride. It is short for Navigator. It is true that this kind of navigator did not hold a master's certificate or stand at the helm on stormy nights. He was a land-animal. But we owe to him some benefits of the water-way, since without him there would have been no internal navigation of Britain.

Our canals were dug, and most valuably at first, for industrial transport at the end of the eighteenth and during the nineteenth century. The men who then and there shaped the conduits for the barges and for Sir Alan Herbert's Water Gypsies were called navigators because they made possible with their spades the work of this mercantile navy of the inland waters. Explorers of our often neglected canals will there discover inns called after the navigators. In them these brawny fellows, toiling without benefit of bull-dozers, and trenching Britain with their gruelling handiwork, slaked their thirst. And there the occasional surviving bargees or holiday amateur of canal-exploration can take his beer still. These may decently raise a glass to the shades of the early navigators who bestowed a title on the later navvies. The latter have no reason to be rid of the abbreviated name as though it were some term of contempt like the odious (and rightly abandoned) slavey and skivvy once applied with a callousness, now fortunately out of date, to women who did the roughest or simplest domestic tasks.

NOSHER

WE are most of us, on occasion, noshers. Reading an article by Mr Guy Deghy .on the pleasures and patrons of delicatessen shops, I learned that noshing is 'sampling food surreptitiously and voluptuously'. The German verb naschen has brought us this term for a slight act of gluttony, slight because sampling suggests the trial mouthful and not the full meal. By using the adverb surreptitiously Mr Deghy did not, I think, imply theft, for his shopkeeper spoke affectionately of the noshers at his counters. Women, the salesman complained, only nosh chocolates and the true nosher is a connoisseur of cheeses at once sharp and ripe, of garlic-flavoured salami, and of those fierce-looking tubes of botulistic 'still life' which decorate the food-store like purple patches in a page of prose. Evidently the salesman's much-liked noshers paid up properly as they nosed and nuzzled and chewed their way from one of his cates to another. Why, by the way, have we almost lost the word cate for a delicacy when caterer is in such common use? I imagined that the cate was a shortened form of delicate but the dictionary maintains that it is short for acate, which is a corruption of the French achète. I wonder.

NUBBINS AND CORN

IN an article, written for an English magazine by an American woman journalist, I noted with sympathy her complaint that after a long day's sightseeing her feet were reduced to nubbins. Nubbins? My sympathy was mixed with curiosity and led to research. These painful articles, so often the product of holiday exercise on ancient, cobbled streets, are strangers to the English language. In America nubbins are 'stunted or dwarfed ears of Indian corn' and therefore, as afflicting a pedestrian, they make a galling synonym for what we call corns.

The queer thing is that our word corn, meaning a thickened piece of skin pressing on the toe or foot, does sound as though it too came from nubbly cereals. But its origin is animal, not vegetable; it is the horny, not the corny growth, derived from the Latin cornus, a horn, which is met with in the word cornucopia: this means the joyous horn of plenty — not a footful of nubbins.

America has sent us another kind of corn. As applied to songs and jokes, corn and corny first indicated something sincere, simple and 'homey'. Then it developed a contemptuous significance and began to imply triteness, staleness and general dreariness. Now, if you see a music-hall turn or a farce described as corny, you are supposed to regard it as rough, over-familiar and tedious. It seems absurd that we should be thus unkind to the primary nourishment of mankind and, by our use of metaphor, treat the staff of life as though it were the symbol of trash.

Meanwhile, I think we might welcome the word nubbins. When I next visit my chiropodist, I shall ask to be de-nubbinated.

The bunion, or protruding and painful toe-joint, caused by a fallen arch, can add substantially to this misery of nubbins. The origin of the word from bunny sounds sufficiently gentle. But the early bunny had nothing to do with Brer Rabbit or the soft and woolly Bunny Dolls. It was old English for a lump caused by a blow.

The melancholy subject of sore feet leads us, as do most investigations of vocabulary, back to the ancient Greeks. The name Oedipus means Swell-foot and was given to this victim of human and divine injustice because he was exposed as a child with his feet bound. His sire, Laius, had been told by an oracle that his son would kill his father and marry his mother. Laius then took defensive action of the most relentless kind. Instead of giving the wretched

child some quick and painless dispatch, he threw him out to die
thus shackled. The boy was rescued but remained a martyr to
swollen feet. (Is the famous part ever acted as a cripple?) So those
who suffer from puffy ankles may be called Oedipeans with no
suggestions, of course, that they are likely to kill or marry their
parents. For relief from our bunions and nubbins we turn to people
also Grecianly named, the chiropodist, specialist in the treatment
of hands and feet, and the pediatrist, the foot-healer, the man who
has the gubbins to deal with nubbins.

ŒUVRE

WHY are the loftiest critics of the arts so fond of calling a man's
works his *œuvre* in the singular? This question occurred to me on
noticing an allusion to the *œuvre* of Bernard Shaw. Art critics are
especially careful to call a painter's output his *œuvre*. Does it mean
more than his works? Opus, of course, can only be used in the single
since opera has been limited to a special kind of drama with music.
(Operas are truly melodramas, since that term originally meant
musical plays, as it should do according to its Greek constituents.
It was inexplicably transformed a long time ago to classify straight
plays of sensational incident and strong emotion whose incidental or
'background' music was by no means essential or even important.)

I became annoyed by the recurrence of the pretentious *œuvre* in
critical articles. Bernard Shaw's writings are better described in the
English language which he wrote with such clarity and force. Let
him be given the works.

ONE-UP-NESS

'ONE-UP-NESS' for extra vitality is now used by Harley Street
doctors when they express their opinions publicly. The metaphor

is from the golf-course. Writing as a golfer who is usually five down and as a victim of low blood-pressure and general inertia, who seems to be always a lot down on his more animated fellows, I deeply envy the one-uppers, the owners of a natural exaltation, the dwellers 'on top of happy hours', the 'pep'-possessed, the jet-propelled.

How does one best cultivate one-up-manship or, better still, that five-up-manship which comes naturally to others? There is alcohol. That has its manifold and manifest pleasures, but sadly defeats its uplifting purpose by leaving the absorbent party in need of more and more doses to sustain the energy just won. One of the Harley Street sages has comforted the addicts (and doubtless satisfied the Distillers' Company) by announcing that whisky is one of the best of pain-killers. But an anaesthetic is not a one-upper.

There are chemical tablets, harmless and beneficial in my experience, which not only enliven but give a more lasting stimulation than alcohol. They are much cheaper than liquor and handier to carry: you cannot conceal a pint-pot in a waistcoat pocket. We are told that such pills are 'habit-forming' and it seems to be always assumed that all habits are bad habits. One does not often hear people praised for forming good habits.

If pep-pills are a bad habit, Five-down-ness is a bad business. The task of getting 'up' and staying there is insoluble without somebody scolding you and snarling about your bad habits. If destiny has made you a 'downer' and incapable of what Field Marshal Montgomery used to call Binge, you can never feel really good unless you are doing something which your pastors, masters and medicos consider really bad.

> Oh, wearisome condition of humanity,
> Born under one law, to another bound.

Fulke Greville, who uttered this sigh, may not have been a one-downer: one can hardly imagine Elizabethans thus reduced despite much affected cosseting of Melancholy. I see them as a high-blood-pressure company with 'upness' taken for granted.

OUTSIDER

NOT long ago a much-discussed book of literary criticism used the word Outsider to classify the type of person who cannot fit into or accept the normal ways of thought and feeling. He is baffled by his own isolation, but not necessarily distressed by it. Peculiar people can enjoy the pleasures of peculiarity; the intellectual rebel can relish driving a harpoon or two into the great whale of normality.

The Outsider will, however, have moments of internal distress. When he takes to writing, as many Outsiders do, he looks out in anger from his solitude and proceeds to turn his inside outside, in order to find relief by this purgation of the emotions with ink and paper and possibly also in order to achieve the often necessary business of earning a living. The 'ornary fellers' have played up quite nicely at times and have obliged the Outsider by reading his books; or at least they have been coaxed by those literary critics who dote on Outsiders into having a dip into the books — using library copies.

My own preference, which betokens, I am assured, a low breed of intelligence, is for the Great Insiders, the writers who may have their moments of despairing isolation but are on the whole happy with all and sundry and can picture, with laughter and with sympathy, the splendours and struggles, the catastrophes and absurdities of the milord and the commoner alike. Shakespeare and Dickens found that ring-side seats gave a satisfactory view of the human circus. They were often angry, but they did not walk out.

Leaving aside the Outsiders with their powerful minds, passions and pens, we have the other Outsider who does not 'belong' socially; he is the target of the snobs who believe that to be different in speech and habits is to be intolerable as a companion or even as an acquaintance. The vocabulary which the snob employs accepts this notion of a social pale which Outsiders must never attempt to cross. There has long been in his conversation a creature called the Bounder, who thinks that gates and pales are there for the jumping.

The word Bounder properly means the man who marks out

limits of territory, a boundary-marker. This kind of bounder might be a politician (or committee of politicians) arranging national and electoral divisions: he might even, I suppose, be the man who marks out the lines of a tennis-court or of a cricket-pitch and the boundaries. But the snob's bounder has won dictionary status as 'a would-be stylish person kept at or beyond the bounds of society'. Such an outsider frequently resents his outer darkness, breaks through bounds, and crashes gates. He is a cad.

Cad is short for caddie, a word once common in Scotland for an odd-job man or porter and later limited, as a rule, to a carrier of golf-clubs. (Owing to the high price of such porterage, this kind of cad has been commonly supplanted by a trundled cart.) The word cad was then transferred to 'an ill-bred fellow or one lacking the finer instincts or feelings'. Now cad has been laughed out of use. A long-popular music-hall turn, presenting a brace of Very Upper Class Gents, had a good deal to do with this, for their constant invocation of the audience with 'Hullo, Cads' became famous. The word 'cad' is not used seriously now for an Outsider, but I suppose that bounder holds on.

When I was a boy in Cheltenham we had a strange word, Oick or Oyik, with which to dismiss those poorer than us or educated at schools deemed inferior to our own. I have had some confirmation from others that it was once in wide use in the middle and west of England. It was a horrid little word and schoolboys can (or could) be horrid little snobs: if it has died out, so much the better.

The general belief that it is right to be well inside, both socially and intellectually, is shown in our use of the word eccentric. This only suggests, in fact, that the despised creature is not quite in the middle. But surely the best brains and characters are not 'dead centre' all the time.

The eccentric used to be called 'a bit dotty'. Now he is loopy, goofy, or round the bend. And why this word 'dotty'? The diction-ary says that it means 'of unsteady gait, caused by stiffness or lameness'. A man thus dotty could hardly be an effective bounder. But he could limp along as an outsider.

F

OVATE

THE musical critic of a daily paper recently reported that a performance was so much enjoyed that 'the audience ovated'. He was challenged by a correspondent in whose opinion this could only mean that the audience laid an egg or deposited a whole clutch of eggs as evidence of its rapture. Since 'to lay an egg' is American slang for to produce a failure in the theatre, to write of the public ovating a success seems unfortunate.

As a matter of fact, the critic was not far wrong. We commonly use ovation for applause and that noun is derived from the Latin verb 'ovare', meaning to rejoice. For some curious reason most of us (the musical critic excepted) have abandoned the verb and kept the noun. There is another ovate, based on the Latin ovum, an egg; this is now an English adjective meaning egg-shaped. It is also, I gather, 'an English equivalent of Welsh, ofydd', and is applied to 'an Eisteddfod graduate of a third order, beside Bard and Druid'. This august species of Celtic ovate is doubtless applauded, if not ovated, for his voice or his verses. It has now become fashionable, under American influence, to drop the long-established word Highbrow and to describe the intellectually pretentious as Egg-heads. The owners of these domes thus provide yet another class of Ovates.

In this matter of applause and ovation, I am now accustomed to seeing the Italian import, furore, entirely misused. A furore used to signify the wild enthusiasm which leads to an ovation. But now it is commonly employed to describe an outburst of rage. The reason is obvious: it looks so much like fury. Many words have changed their meanings because of their looks. Fruition is a good example. It properly means enjoyment, as in 'The sweet fruition of an earthly crown'. But it has a fruity aspect and it is now almost universally used to imply fertility and ripeness. A stickler for verbal accuracy would say of a much applauded or 'ovated' actor or singer that he had the fruition of a furore. This would certainly not mean that he got 'the screaming bird' or, as the Victorians said, was 'goosed', i.e. hissed: it would imply that he enjoyed his 'round' (of cheers) or got several curtains. But in my reading of popular newspapers furore is far more often used of hostile uproar than of friendly acclamation.

Postscript: The President of the U.S.A., while discussing one of the ever recurring international crises, has just spoken of the furore in Moscow. He was not suggesting that Russia was in a frenzy of praise for all things Western and eager to ovate the policies of Washington; far from it.

OVERALL

PEOPLE who like to see words used properly often point out the absurd misuse of over-all, now usually printed overall, without the hyphen, whereby it has assumed the functions of the adjectives general, inclusive and total. In *The ABC of Plain Words* Sir Ernest Gowers has tabulated some of the meanings of the popular overall recently noticed by him. They are aggregate, altogether, total, average, supreme, on the whole, generally, overriding, comprehensive and whole. To call a Supreme Commander an overall commander seems justifiable, but to talk of 'houses at an overall density of three to the acre' is ridiculous. What is wrong with average? Even sillier is to describe the total runs made by a cricket team in one innings as its 'overall score'. Has it defeated every team in the world? 'Overall profits' are now continually occurring in chairmen's speeches to shareholders. What these chairmen are describing are the total or inclusive profits of the year's trading. But they must be fashionable and drag in the favourite overall. By doing so they surely imply that they have defeated all other companies in amassing profits.

Sir Ernest Gowers says of the favour shown to overall, 'it is an egregious example of the habit of preferring a novel word of vague import to established words of precise meaning: indeed the word seems to have a quality that impels people to use it in settings in which it has no meaning at all'.

It may seem fantastic, but I believe that this impelling quality inherent in overall is the presence of sonority, almost of poetry, in its composition. In previous Word Books I have commented on the emotional power of the letters 'o' and 'r' when found in combination. Rome sounds eternal in strength and Rose sounds ageless in beauty in a way that Athens and Lily do not. Tennyson's 'Glory of warrior, glory of orator, glory of song' fades into nothingness if it be altered to 'Fame of soldier, fame of speaker, fame of verse'. A good sequence of 'O's' and 'R's' carries a poet well on his way if he is ready to consider the more obvious kinds of overall effect. To roll overall from the back of the mouth to the lips is much more satisfactory than to eject total through the teeth.

So that company chairman, expounding the encouraging figures in the balance sheet, can really enjoy himself as he talks of his overall instead of total or general profits. He has no intention of claiming that his company has out-reached all others in the making of gains. He is just yielding to the fascination of a labial letter. Total does contain the long 'o', but its dental quality makes it far less cosy in the mouth than the sonorous overall. The latter richly creates the background music for a larger dividend.

PAY OFF

THE desire to add one or more prepositions to a verb seems to be insatiable, however foolish the result. The silliness of 'meet up with', which does not mean more than meet, is an obvious example. Sometimes this itch for unnecessary syllables actually betrays the sense. I rarely read now of a policy that pays and frequently of a policy that pays off. Why the off? To pay a man off is to be rid of an unwanted employee. So a policy which pays off should be a failure implying dismissal. The phrase surely indicates that the framer of the policy has done poorly and might himself be paid off.

If we must have an added preposition, pay out would make much better sense. But why have any addition? 'His policy paid' has a clear meaning to me, whether applied to a statesman or the captain of a team engaged in a game. There is no point whatever in saying that the policy paid off. But one constantly meets this irritating folly: or rather, to write à la mode, one constantly 'meets up with it'.

PRESERVES

MOST branches of life have their own lingo. The country hotel, whose cooking is as English as a dollop of wet cabbage, advertises, along with its 'blazing log fires', 'superb cuisine'. The results of this may be served in 'the coffee room' though the coffee, which may or may not earn that name, is not served there at all, but in 'the lounge'. (A London club of my acquaintance calls its dining-room its Coffee Room, although coffee is the last and least of the liquors usually taken there. After lunch the more replete and leisurely members retire for purposes of sleep to what is called the Morning Room, although, since it is not a residential club, there will be nobody there in the morning, and quite a crowd in the afternoon.)

The hotel with 'superb cuisine' will certainly conclude its breakfast menu with 'Preserves'. Is this word ever employed in an ordinary English home? Does the husband inquire of the wife, 'What have we in the way of preserves?' It can be argued that Preserves is a useful term since it covers jam, marmalade and honey for which there is no other group name. As a matter of fact and experience, the obtaining of anything but marmalade at an hotel breakfast is apt to be quite a business. Marmalade is there on the table: it is assumed that everybody dotes on marmalade: and those who would prefer honey or jam must catch the attention of a distant and occupied waiter or waitress. If they are at length successful in that, they must then wait some time while that waiter or waitress, annoyed by this show of fussiness, goes away and reluctantly rummages for the required article. But as the years go by nothing dislodges Preserves from our hotel vocabulary.

To me the word suggests great Victorian sideboards, huge cruets and gigantic 'repasts'. I am too old now to want a matutinal repast. But hungry schoolboys on holiday do. The hotel of today, preserving its menu-title of Preserves, considers that one egg with a scrap of bacon or half a grilled tomato makes what is called a Full Breakfast. Without demanding the old massive breakfast, with a fish course (several choices) before the eggs and bacon, we may reasonably remind the hotelier of today that nobody in my youth ever talked of or considered 'egg and bacon' or 'ham and egg'. The plural was taken for granted in the matter of eggs. To serve one would have proclaimed an inferior and niggardly house, unless there were several other courses.

Between 1939 and 1945 eggs were, except in a few remote and rustic spots, absentees, and preserves too were scarce enough. No grumbling then. But I fail to see why bacon and eggs should not now be restored with the latter in their proper plural, or at least dual, form. I have been in country towns recently where the shops were full of eggs at summer prices, say threepence halfpenny. The hotel charged six shillings for breakfast — a price which might be thought to cover a second egg. But the proprietor had no ideas of that kind, just as he had no idea that one can like marmalade well enough without liking it every morning in the year.

PROBLEM

OWING to the political, economic and various psychological difficulties of our time Problem has become one of the commonest English words. In the Press, in debates and discussions, printed or broadcast, and in ordinary conversation it is a case of problems, problems all the way. The word problem has a Greek origin. The verb 'ballein' meant to throw; the ancient 'problema' was a thing thrown forward, especially a thing projected as a good subject for

academic discussion. (The Latin project represents the same idea —
a thing thrown — but projects have become purposes while problems remain puzzles.) Our ball is also something thrown about, but
the dictionaries do not associate it with the Greek 'ballein'; they
speak instead of early Norse and Teutonic forms, such as böllr.
However that may be, when the chairman now says to a member
of the discussion-group, 'I am passing the ball to you', he is handing
over the oldest kind of problem, the article tossed forward.

This hard-worked problem has now become as odious as common. Most corners of the map have a racial problem, only soluble
if mankind will grow up, be sensible and abandon homicidal
squabbling over patches of sand. Such a solution mankind is apparently quite unable or unwilling to provide. This kind of problem
existed in Hamlet's time: it was the Danish–Norwegian problem
then. 'The imminent death of twenty thousand men' was threatened
by strife over a plot of land 'not tomb enough and continent to hide
the slain', a massacre for an egg-shell. Shakespeare did not speak of
a problem: he was fortunate. He did not know, or at least never
used, the now inescapable word which is the source of such endless
and wearisome disputations, brawls and bloodshed. What food
for endless speech could the Assembly of the United Nations find
without the incessant dilemmas of our pro-ballistic world?

From problem we have created problematical to describe what
is questionable or untrue. We have also played our usual trick of
turning the noun into an adjective. So the 'bold unbiddable boy'
and the girl described as 'mixed-up' have become Problem Children.
Hamlet, whose play has posed so many problems to the professors
that many shelves of a library could be filled with books on Hamlet
only, might now be described as the Problem Prince.

PROPOSITIONING

'IT is as easy', said Shakespeare's Celia to Rosalind, 'to count
atomies as to resolve the proposition of a lover.' What exactly did

she mean? Not, I fancy, what is signified by the dreadful word 'propositioning' which has lately been added to the English lexicon of Eros.

In an amusing novel which recently recounted the lives and loves of up-to-date young women (*The Cost of Living* by Kathleen Farrell) I noted the mention of 'propositioning types'. These, I gathered, are men who make the kind of advances once deemed improper. There is thus a nice distinction between a proposal, which implies marriage, and a proposition, which does not. Proposal was a good, solid Victorian term for honourable popping of the question. But we may wonder whether John Donne had only respectable courtship in mind when he sourly observed,

> Whosoever loves, if he do not propose
> The right true end of love, he's one that goes
> To sea for nothing but to make him sick.

However, proposing settled down as the ethical approach to the tying of the sacred knot.

> Why don't the men propose, Mamma,
> Why don't the men propose?

This plaintive query occurs in one of the popular ballads which came from the prolific pen of Thomas Haynes Bayley who, in a short life (1797-1839) enriched our minstrelsy with 'She Wore A Wreath of Roses'; 'Gaily the Troubadour'; 'We met, t'was in a crowd and I thought he would shun me'; and 'Absence makes the heart grow fonder'.

Bayley did not sing of the sinister 'propositioners' who have supplanted the previous practitioners of 'dating'.

There is certainly no romance in this polysyllable chunk of Latinity and, if a girl tells you that she met a Propositionist last night, it hardly suggests by its sound a Sports Car Lochinvar or an expert in the persuasive phrasing of admiration and seduction. Presumably it is the American influence that inflicts these formidable classicisms on us; American word-usage favours either the very short or the very long. Either a Wolf makes a pass at a Dame or a Propositionist decisions to prospect for a Sophisticate. (See note on Sophisticated.) But the life of sexual encounter in the U.S.A. could once be carried on with monosyllables. They 'mashed' instead of 'propositioned'.

The Americans wrote 'Limericks' as far back as 1879. Here is one of them:

> There was a young man of New Haven
> Who always was smoothly shaven.
> Without a moustache
> He never could mash
> The girls, who thought him a craven.

That was poor stuff, with a second line that does not properly scan. But it is interesting as evidence that our young men with 'handlebars' would have been much favoured in New Haven about eighty years ago; interesting also for its employment of the word 'mash', which was once much used of glamorous actors who so mashed their public as to get a 'mash-mail', as fan-mail was then called.

English writers have used 'mash', even of perfect gentlemen. Kipling's descriptions of love in a hot climate include much mashing, but dishonourable intentions were not implied. When the young officers on leave in Simla went quite respectably wooing and wiving they were described as mashers. Even that unbearably perfect specimen of the English officer and gentleman, Bobby Wick of *Only a Subaltern*, went mashing the Haverley girl. But mashing sank in the world: it became no better than spooning and now both these nasty little words, familiar in the concert party lingo of my boyhood, have disappeared.

What have we in their place? Wooing and courting are 'period pieces'. Making a pass at? But that suggests malpractice. Bobby Wick would never have made passes — except at football. When I read about the mashing officers in Kipling I shudder at the word, but what have we in its place to suggest a young man's gay, yet not licentious, pursuit of the sweet and fair? Subaltern Wick may have mashed and even spooned; he would never have propositioned.

Our own North Country, I am reminded, has its own words for the conduct of a courtship — and very simple they are. A Propositionist is surely flattered when he is called 'ower fond' and better named 'a warm 'un'. A proposal of the honest kind was thus once made: 'Say, lass, if I said traycle [treacle], would you be willing to lick?' The result, it seems, was an acceptance of the syrup and a very happy marriage.

PROVERBIALLY

'ARTISTS proverbially are poor business men.' This from a letter to *The Times*. Is it a true statement? Of course there have been feckless fellows in studio and study. So have there been chuckle-heads in business itself. Carey Street is not the sad resort of Chelsea folk alone. Many authors and artists have been sharp enough, and writers have frequently extorted from publishers, even without an agent's aid, advance royalties which were never subsequently earned: sometimes the book was never written at all. Some publishers are sanguine fellows.

But, even if we agree about the improvidence of artists, why throw in the adverb 'proverbially'? Is there any well-known proverb concerning lack of financial acumen in those who follow the arts? 'A fool and his money are soon parted.' No doubt, but artists are not always fools. Here is another example of the use of this now favoured adverb: a City editor writes, 'First-class Trust shares are proverbially scarce'. What ancient wiseacre composed a proverb about Trust shares?

What is a proverb? 'A short pithy saying in common use, an adage, a wise saw.' (A saw, oddly, is the same word as saga, the thing said, but the brevity of the former is the opposite of the prolixity of the latter.) Thomas Fuller called a proverb 'much matter decocted into a few words'. This decoction may be a quotation which has been so much used (with its source so much forgotten) that it is now regarded as an anonymous piece of common sense. In this way, many a line of Shakespeare's has become proverbial. Or the proverb may have come into acceptance as a neat phrase for some result of general observation and agreement. But there is no certainty of agreement. It has been noted that proverbs cancel each other out. One advocates the advantages of prudence. We must look before we leap. Another affirms the need of immediacy and audacity. We must strike while the iron is hot: we must take time by the forelock: we must be timely with our stitches. The proverb has its sundry (and conflicting) qualities of good sense. But now, as the letter quoted above demonstrates, proverbially has come to mean no more than often or as a rule.

Adverbs, especially long ones, have a habit of becoming suddenly, and infuriatingly, fashionable. At one time 'definitely' was the favourite. Smart talkers used it when they only meant to say 'yes'. 'Will you be in tomorrow?' 'Definitely.' At the time of writing 'actually' is one of the favourites. I met some young people recently who used 'actually' in almost every sentence. 'Are you living in London?' 'Actually, I am.' 'Actually we must be going now.'

Actually, I did not mind if they did.

PSEPHOLOGIST

EVER since there were politicians and elections there must have been students of the voting methods and their results. But this exercise has only recently been raised to the status of a science and practised by academic figures in the Universities. With a curious pedantry these sages have adopted, or have been given by other pedants, a sonorous classical title. If asked in one of our broadcast programmes what is their line, they would say, 'Psephology'.

That is Greek indeed to the ordinary voter. The Greek word 'psephos' meant a pebble and one of the earliest forms of voting was the casting of pebbles into one receptacle or another. So the psephologist, after being a counter of pebbles or an observer of the pebble-throwers, has come to be an expert examiner of modern ballots and what they prove. The votes cast at one of our General Elections are tabulated and analysed with regard to previous results, changes of population, and so on, in order to chart movements of opinion. So from the original stone-throwing we derive our new science of Psephology.

The nearest surviving thing to the primitive Psephos or Psepho-ballistics (pebble-casting) is surely the Black Ball, still in use for exclusive purposes in clubs whose members are determined to keep 'outsiders' outside. When candidates are up for election, there are black balls available for objecting members of the committee to throw into the ballot-box, along with balls of other colour signify-ing approval.

My friend, Arthur Ransome, gave me a delightful Latin alter-native name for this sport of the scrupulous committee-man, Nigroglobulation. If Greek be still preferred, the Nigroglobulist, or black-baller, can be called a Melanopsephist, melas being the Greek for black. That adjective is conspicuous in our word melan-choly, which means blackness of the bile and the emotional state supposed to be produced by this sad discoloration. Black-ballers at elections may well be suffering from such bilious derangement and in need of a choliagogue. The latter word I have discovered on the label of a bottle of pills: the 'agogue' part of it is derived from the Greek for a guide or leader, as in demagogue, leader of the people. A choliagogue is thus a stimulant of the bile, its conveyor into the right quarter, and an improver of our colour-scheme.

Psephology is a new-comer, but another Greek voting-term has long been with us. This is 'ostracize'. The Athenians had the idea that a demagogue who was becoming over-important, tyrannical and 'too big for his sandals' might well be dispensed with: but the process of dismissal was democratic and merciful. ('Liquidation' of the ambitious or deviating statesman is a more recent and ruthless form of political dismissal and is much favoured in Totalitarian

States.) The 'ostracon' was a tile or potsherd on which was written the name of the man supposed to merit exile from Athens for a stated period of years. A vote was taken and the citizen who received enough of these electoral brick-bats was then ordered to quit. This odd, and often salutary as well as humane method of dealing with a public nuisance, has given us the word ostracism, which now denotes cold-shouldering and social exclusion, instead of actual banishment.

Discussion of voting and its vocabulary leads me from pebbles and tiles to pots and pans. Here is a relevant extract from the minor news of a year ago.

> Recent achievements of the 'pot-wallopers' of Hatherleigh, commoners of a North Devon market-town, occupied the grave attention of the Royal Commission on Common Land at their public hearing of evidence in London.

Who and why are pot-wallopers? The Hatherleigh folk who are thus described had recovered the grazing rights in a common which had been ploughed up for food-growing in war-time. They did not intend to lose their ancient pasture, which is all in the way of human nature and of English tenacity in our way of country life. But what has this to do with the walloping of pots or the potting of wallops? The latter certainly suggests a happy and liberal absorption of mild ale.

The explanation, however, is not so convivial. A pot-walloper appears to be an elongated version of pot-waller. The Anglo-Saxon verb 'wall' meant, in its time, 'to boil'. So a pot-waller was a man with his own fireplace and his own fire for keeping the pot a-boil. Before the Reform Act of 1832 a householder was deemed to be a man of substance and so qualified as an elector if he had his own fireplace and did his own pot-walling. Wallop was a popular alteration of wall and hence the pot-walloper was a citizen with a fireplace, a pot to boil on it, and the consequent electoral status. Hence, in the eyes of Hatherleigh today, the pot-walloper is a man with agrarian as well as political rights and is entitled to put his own cow on the common. The pot-boilers of old England were the equivalent of the pebble-throwing Greeks and so raw material for the psephologists of their time, had that profession then arisen.

PURLIEU AND PURVIEW

I WAS mildly surprised, when reading an American book about London, to find my suburb of Hampstead described as 'an art and culture purlieu'. True, we of N.W.3 do have some odd-looking types who presumably wish to show their height of brow by their depth of personal squalor. But purlieu? I thought it was a word of contempt, signifying a slum. So it was to Charles Lamb who wrote sadly of 'the purlieus of Bethnal Green'. But my American was right, for the earliest kind of English (or Anglo-French) purlieu was the land surrounding a forest. Ascot, in this case, is a purlieu of Windsor Park. But this word for the outskirts of a forest also became the word for the outskirts of a town. Then, because the edges, now called by pompous people the perimeter, of a town are often rather shabby, purlieu became a term of discredit. Nobody would describe himself as living in a purlieu but, as a matter of fact, he would be asserting residence in some agreeably rural spot.

Purview is now a somewhat lofty term for range of vision or field of labour. One expects the most exalted kind of Civil Servant, reigning in the higher purlieus of Whitehall, to tell us that a question or complaint is outside his purview when he means that it is not his job or worry. Originally purview was an Anglo-French term. It meant 'provided that' and was used in legal documents and statutes. When its origin was forgotten, purview came to mean the scope of the document or legislation.

Despite the misfortunes that overcame the word purlieu there remains something haughty about the words beginning with pur. Purchase is lordlier than buy and to be a purveyor is much more imposing than to be a mere seller. Purloin, furthermore, is an extremely polite variant for steal or pinch. That courtly and heraldic fellow a Pursuivant would never buy his tea and sugar from a grocer. He would purchase from a purveyor who had such wares in his purview.

RANNYGAZOO

I CAME across a rannygazoo, explained as 'funny business', in a new book by P. G. Wodehouse, entitled *Something Fishy*. (Is there a verb rannygazoogle? It would rank nicely with hornswoggle and honeyfuggle which are both American terms for bamboozle.) One word leads to another. Why bamboozle? Nobody knows. It was, according to Dean Swift, 'struggling for the vogue' in his time. In America it did not originally have the meaning we give it, that of swindling. To be bamboozled was first to be jostled about and then intoxicated. Perhaps because simple folk are pushed about or robbed over a drink or two, the American bamboozler, like ours, came later on to signify one engaged in something fishy, a ranny-gazoogler. Fishy became, I suppose, synonymous with crooked because fish are slippery or because, after a time, fish stinks. This is most unfair. There are, it is true, evil-looking fish, and some terrifying specimens goggle at one through the glass in an aquarium. But what more innocent than a portion of halibut? A turbot may sound pompous, but surely it has a nature pure as snow.

Wodehouse also uses the American plug-ugly; this fellow was more of a rough than a practitioner of rannygazoo. The plug-uglies are historic figures: they intervened with violence on the side of slavery in the Kansas struggle of a century ago. They lived on to intimidate voters and strikers. Hornswoggling and honeyfuggling, like rannygazoo, imply some use of wits. Plug-uglies need not have brains, provided the brawn is there — and probably a weapon too.

RELAXED

RELAXED has recently become an inescapable item in the reporter's vocabulary. The Great, when interviewed and questioned about the causes of their eminence, are no longer described as calm, smiling, or contented. They are always relaxed. Interviewers are great users of vogue-adjectives, of which relaxed is now the chief. Interviewed persons, when young and tall, are inevitably gangling, which I take to mean loose-limbed, or balding and chunky, if they are solidly built seniors, short of hair. 'Relaxed in his roof-garden balding, chunky Sir Midas told me yesterday of the fabulous success of his new venture.' (I am beginning to ache at the sight of fabulous.) It is evidence of the tension of our times that the height of our happiness is no positive ecstasy but a negative freedom from strain. The summit of bodily health is not to be actively abounding in vigour but merely to have escaped, so far, the crisis of nerves and the almost universal ulcer. In my note on Cerebrotonic I had something to say of the new tight-lacing of the mind. Relaxed Sir Midas has his brain-laces comfortably slack about his money-spinning cranium.

Here is an adjective which has largely changed its meaning. Relaxing and relaxed used to be terms of dispraise. Charlotte Brontë wrote of 'a weak and relaxed character' to signify her disdain of flabbiness and laziness. There was once a strong dislike of relaxing places. 'Bath is delightful to look at, but too relaxing for me.' Many of our educational centres, being sited on rivers, have been naturally approved for stimulus of the eye and deplored for their softness and mugginess of climate. Educated at Cheltenham, in its agreeable but often airless niche in the Cotswolds, and at Oxford, with its river-mists, I have myself known climatic relaxation to the full. Luckily the young are less subject to the lassitude of low-lying places than are their elders. But now relaxing localities should be extremely popular, since they provide a full antidote to cerebrotony. If I were being interviewed I would rather be called alert than relaxed, but in that case I should be out of fashion.

William Blake's apophthegm, 'Damn braces. Bless relaxes', was an incitement to curse and swear as the proper stimulant of sluggish men. He did not view the relaxed citizen as a good example of euphoria. I introduce the latter word because it has become a favourite of the intellectuals who prefer a classic to a Saxon word. It means no more than well-being and I can see no reason for airing one's Greek when all that is intended is a description of general happiness. The simple word 'well-being' is well enough and needs no bettering.

Soon after writing the above I noticed that Relaxed was honoured with a Fourth leader in *The Times*. The writer noted that a word once mainly used to describe a sore throat had become a form of highest commendation in the animal world as well as that of *homo* supposedly *sapiens*. The Derby winner of 1957, Crepello, was praised for being relaxed in the paddock before he triumphantly displayed his readiness for a braced-up exercise. In the arenas of human sport the entrants to whom this vogue-word is applied are usually champions. I have seen a report of a long sculling race, that for Doggett's Coat and Badge, in which the winner's victory was attributed to his being so relaxed as he proceeded down the course. To be relaxed before setting forth on a 'needle' round of golf would have sounded dangerously slack in the old days when it was customary to picture competitors as arriving full of 'pep' and on their toes. Now they are thought to be in the best of form if they yawn in the face of the Press cameras and can be verbally pictured as perfectly relaxed. To the seniors, relaxed may still suggest an old gentleman with a wheezy chest and sore throat dozing in a Bath Chair at one of our drowsier Spas. But now it is the sovereign runner, rower, or smiter of the ball who earns the easeful epithet.

RUMBUNCTIOUS

I NOTE in my evening paper that Sir Albert Richardson, late President of the Royal Academy, is described as rumbunctious. It is not a word favoured by the compilers of dictionaries, but an American form, rambunctious, is admitted and given an age of about a century.

Rumbustion was an old, slang name for rum, and rumbustious is therefore a fair adjective for fiery-tempered and free-spoken persons. Rambunctious fellows suggests oncoming, head-down, butting, damn-you-ram-you characters. With rumbunctious we get back to the Yo-ho-ho company and 'the old, bold mates of Henry Morgan'. But why rumbunctious rather than rumbustious? There was no indication that Sir Albert was talking 'bunk' or that the epithet need suggest folly in any way. It simply describes the opposite of mealy-mouthed. The man to whom it is applied is evidently pictured as swilling strong spirit round his mouth and so liberated from cautious inhibitions instead of being clogged with the sticky fodder of a too mannerly precaution.

To return to Sir Albert, he did not appear, on the occasion mentioned, to be earning the violent adjective in any desperate manner. He was only denouncing the destruction of old buildings in his own town of Ampthill and the construction of concrete lamp-posts, which he dismissed with the now frequent adjective 'sub-topian'. Of subtopianism more is said under its own name.

SATELLITE

SHAKESPEARE'S Puck promised to put a girdle round the earth in forty minutes. The Moscow satellite, Red Moon, or Bleeper, which took the non-Russian world by surprise in October 1957, did not quite make Puck's grade of orbital celerity. But it was not far behind.

The word satellite comes from the classics. It described a personal servant or guard waiting on a figure of rank or importance. The major type of satellite, when the word was taken over from the Latin, was a constant follower and possibly a biographer. In the eighteenth century Boswell was called Johnson's satellite. Dr Watson was later an admirable satellite to Sherlock Holmes. Two humbler, but most effective satellites, rarely found failing to cope, were Mr Pickwick's Sam Weller and Bertie Wooster's Jeeves.

Satellites, beginning in the guard room or servant's hall, soared to literary status. In the same way the word soared into the skies where it has been applied to secondary planets revolving round primary ones. The moon is our astronomical attendant in this class.

Soviet Russia is a great manufacturer of satellites, on earth as in the skies. It has its ring of satellite states, which are by no means willing servants but more or less captive bodies controlled by the Great Power. The space-free revolutions of a heavenly satellite are denied to the subject peoples. Revolution is a luxury limited to Russia.

We have also, in our lingo of town-planning, satellite towns. They are small towns outside a big one and probably attached to it economically. Space-fiction and the possible experiments in spatial penetration have involved further uses of the old word for companion or bodyguard. A satellite station is (or will be) a construction, possibly habitable, launched into space and moving in an orbit round a planetary body. It will be used by the mariners of space-ships as a kind of supply-base while these heroes are rocketed farther into the vast unknown. One can only hope that these satellite stations will be as helpful to their users as were the earliest satellites, the sedulous valets, custodians and counsellors who pressed their masters' clothes, smoothed their masters' tempers, ironed out their masters' problems, or, at the highest Boswellian or Watsonian level, were the recorders and diarists of the planetary figures whom they followed in eighteenth-century discourse or nineteenth-century detection.

SATISFIED

ACCORDING to Mr V. H. Collins, author of *Right Word, Wrong Word*, and many other excellent books on language and its treatment, the use of satisfied to mean convinced of a fact or convinced by a theory has a respectable antiquity. But it can sound ridiculous when applied to objectionable or horrible things. He quotes from America, 'the man's family is satisfied that he was murdered', which suggests to us a queer form of contentment. But the English can be equally strange in their references to satisfaction. I have noted that an English town's Medical Officer of Health, discussing a 'polio' outbreak, said that he was 'satisfied that the local river was heavily polluted with sewage'.

To satisfy means, literally, to make enough or to give a feeling of sufficiency. Enough of what? Not only of food and drink, which leaves a diner satisfied instead of surfeited, but also of information to meet the examiners' requirements, of money to meet a claim, or of penalty to reward a crime. Generally, however, satisfaction carries the implication of some pleasure. But now we can be satisfied with news, even of the most noisome kind. This is due, I think, to a quirk of official usage. The Minister for this or that continually answers a Parliamentary question or complaint by announcing that he is satisfied that all is, officially, being done for the best by the best of all possible Departments. Then the idea of good news drops out and the satisfaction can be applied to bad news. Hence we can be satisfied to learn that one of our famous English rivers is no better than a filthy and most insanitary drain.

I used the adjective noisome of such news, remembering that annoy is a word that once had a much stronger meaning than that of petty vexation. Milton wrote of sewers that annoy the air. He was far from being satisfied thereat.

SIC

Sic is the Latin for thus and is often used in brackets and contemptuously by critics and commentators when they have found a misprint or an error in somebody's writing. They quote the mistake and put [sic] after it, to show that they, the writers, being clever and learned, are well aware of the blunder. If, for example, in the book in question, the name of Disraeli happened to be printed Dizraeli, the reviewer would loftily cite the passage and write 'Dizraeli [sic]'.

Why not 'thus' instead of 'sic'? Snobbery is as powerful in the matter of lingo as it is of lineage. So Latinisms, born of a desire to show signs of a classical education, hang on. Many of them are absurd. One sees theatres advertising 'Gigantic Success. Vide Press'. Vide is a singular Latin imperative, meaning See Thou, and obviously the appeal is to more than one potential playgoer. So Videte, See Ye, would make a little more sense, but not much more, since the 'Press' to be seen was yesterday's or last week's which has presumably been tidied away.

No accused person tries to prove 'an elsewhere'. He sticks to Latin and puts up an alibi. The word alibi has become so popular that it is now taken to mean an excuse of any kind, without reference to place. This usage has now reached the front benches of the House of Commons where the word alibi is commonly employed to mean explanation. A stickler for correctness would doubtless play the 'sic' trick and phrase his report or comment thus: 'In answer to questions in the House the Minister for Evasion stated that he had a complete and perfect alibi [sic].'

The sound of 'sic' suggests the haughty dismissal of an error so gross as to be nauseous. It can be uttered in a very desiccated [dry] tone of voice.

SIGNIFICS

THE death in March 1957 of C. K. Ogden, founder of Basic English, reminded me that, when I was a member of an undergraduates' philosophical society at Oxford, Ogden came over from Cambridge to talk to us on what he called Significs. He argued that any study of philosophy was made absurdly difficult for the general public by the vagueness of the terms employed and that it had become a necessary academic discipline to clean up this muddle of vocabulary. We were to establish a code of Significs which would enable us to understand clearly what was being conveyed by words at present employed with a series of different meanings. I think we all agreed with Ogden about the need for clarification. His pleas, like most pleas which are fully justified, were applauded — and forgotten. The old confusion remains to confound.

Our philosophers still continue to use the word idealism to indicate a metaphysical theory about the nature of the universe and also a moral and psychological theory about ethical goals and the possible betterment, even the perfectibility, of human nature. These two doctrines have nothing in common except their name. The same holds true of the opposite of idealism. Realism is applied to a metaphysical theory about the nature of things and to an intellectual and psychological attitude to the nature of man and his behaviour. Furthermore, realism has now been given a fresh and sinister political meaning. The early realists begged us to abandon what they deemed to be our illusions; the later ask us, in the name of this reality, to abandon all decency. A realistic policy, to a Communist, is another name for a ruthless one. In a short book called *English Gone Wrong* Mr Eric Partridge, in discussing the abuse of this word, reminds us that Lord Samuel had said in 1937, 'Name it "realism" and any wickedness becomes allowable'. How true that remains.

Next, there is the use of the word realism in discussions on Art. This realism is sometimes called naturalism, which implies that the artist is treating the things which he paints or carves or describes in words with a considerable approximation to perceived fact. The realist is not and should not be a mere copyist: but neither is he a devotee of distortion or abstraction, submitting his subject entirely to his own ideas of interpretation.

Ogden's idea of coded Significs, a word now partially supplanted by Semantics, was never taken up. His Basic English had the blessing of political authority during the Second World War, but did not make a wide appeal. It is a curious fact that, while the differences and the complexities of many languages and the difficulty of mastering more than a few of them remain as a pestilent public nuisance, efforts to get rid of the trouble make no progress. Basic English, by reducing our widely spoken tongue to its simplest elements, should have encouraged a much commoner study of English and its adoption in basic form as a language of cosmic range. But has it? I once acquired a little of the easily learned Esperanto, but found no occasion to use it and soon forgot it. It seems that Babel is, and will remain, a very popular Tower. Languages give a lot of trouble, but we are too lazy to take the trouble to cope with trouble.

One department of life especially needs an intelligent application of Significs. That is the world of the artist who, whatever his medium, seems quite content with a series of -isms which are usually meaningless without definition and lead to arguments which are futile. It is simple and it is imposing to rap out a longish word; the listener or reader is expected to be impressed and to believe that the artist or the critic of the arts really has some clear and easily explained meaning in mind when he talks of this or that portentous -ism. When looking back at the -isms that have been modish in my time, I remember a few that were reasonable and helpful and many more that were not.

I began my aesthetic studies with the vague and silly chatter of the Vorticist cult. Its juvenile pioneers were Wyndham Lewis and Ezra Pound and its whirlwind doctrine was expounded in a magazine called *Blast*. Post-Impressionism had then followed Impressionism: the latter had a recognizable meaning, but the former had not. One, however, of the Post-Impressionist departments was simply and accurately entitled Cubism, since the artist in this case reduced the world of his vision to a series of rectangular solids. After that came a stream of supposedly dynamic doctrines, Vitalism, Dadaism, Expressionism and so forth. Since all art must express something, Expressionism was a term so inclusive as to be quite useless. In the theatre, for example, Expressionism became a covering term for almost any play or production that was not realistic in its stage-craft and technique.

Later we had Constructivism, which meant the abandonment of normal scenery for an assortment of packing-cases and ladders. More recently Existentialism, a term drawn from philosophy, has found its way into the arts and more especially of those practitioners and critics of the arts who dote on a thumping long word without bothering at all as to its meaning. Philosophic Existentialism, according to one authority 'holds the individual responsible for what he is, assuming that the individual is both contingent and free. Protesting against the indifference of this contingent yet free individual Existentialism developed after the Second World War into a pessimistic philosophy which holds that the individual must oppose his hostile environment by exercising his free will'. (Reifer's *Dictionary of New Words*.)

That may, or may not, have dissolved the mist in front of the students' eyes. (I am not clear myself as to the exact meaning of 'contingent' in this connection — but let that pass.) What is obvious is that this kind of anti-determinist ethical doctrine has nothing to do with theatrical method. Yet I have heard a theatrical director announce that he was about to offer us an Existentialist production of a play. After giving him some polite cross-examination I found that he had merely picked on Existentialist as a vogue-word which would give him the status of an intellectual. What he sought to imply was that he would give a non-realistic presentation. He seemed to think that Existentialist was a synonym for Surrealist. People of this kind should have been sent to school with C. K. Ogden and not let out until they qualified in Significs.

SKEDADDLE

It was odd to find Skedaddle appearing again. To me it was a childhood term. Authority calls it 'old American military slang' and certainly it is sufficiently descriptive of a hurried retreat. Now, in the common vocabulary of departure, its place has been taken by scarper. This, I understand, is an example of that cockney rhyming slang which I am not alone in regarding as tiresome and silly. Go rhymes with flow: therefore Scapa Flow means go: and Scapa in the lingo of the children's 'comic' and the strip-cartoon is written Scarper. Scram is presumably just scramble abbreviated. 'Beat it' holds on. It was Elizabethan slang in its own time. 'Come, let us beat it down the cobbled street' made good sense with its suggestion of the ringing hoof or clattering heel.

The Elizabethans also had shog, a form of jog, in their vocabulary of dismissals and departures. 'Shog off' was their terse and vigorous alternative to our 'get a move on'.

To quit, a short form of acquit, first meant to release and continued to do so for centuries: a man could be quitted of a charge, a crime, or a punishment. At last the transitive verb became, first in America, intransitive. So the prisoner, being quitted in the old sense, now quitted the dock in the new. Finally quit became a common usage in the scarper and skedaddle class of verbs, frequently used in the imperative way.

Skiddoo has the skedaddle sound. This word has not, I think, found any strong lodgment in English. But the American *Century Magazine* stated in 1929 that a quarter of a century ago skiddoo had been 'on everybody's tongue'. The magazine added: 'It was the equivalent of the more modern invitation to "take the air" and was generally used in speeding the unwelcome guest.' As a command to skedaddle, skiddoo has merits and should be a help in banishing the unruly child who is making a nuisance of himself. I do not see it being effective against larger pests.

SKIFFLE

SKIFFLE groups established themselves in Britain during 1956. They were teams of three or four who played assorted instruments, often of a home-made kind. The corrugated wash-board was one of them, but genuine guitars were important. Skiffle, an expert skiffler informed me, came from the rustic American plains, not the mountains: the prairie-billies, not the hill-billies, invented it. The melodies favoured were more folksy than frantic. Skiffle groups were liked in places frequented by the young, such as the Espresso cafés much used by those who found alcoholic drinks unachievable in any rewarding quantity for reasons of cost. None of the castigators of public morals had, at the time this was written, indicted skiffle as satanic. Some skifflers seemed able to work themselves up from the plain song to the wildly percussive and to reach the state of perspiration and exaltation that marked the 'monarchs' of jazz and jive. But, for the most part, skiffle was not, at first, ecstatic in its effects.

My specialist told me that skiffle would soon be on its way out. How rapidly fashions in popular music change was exemplified for me by a boy who had been given some Christmas money which he spent on gramophone records. When asked what records he had got for himself, he replied, in one word, 'Traditional'. One might have thought that he had gone in search of England's tuneful past and had come back with a store of madrigals and glees. Had he been entranced by flouting Phyllida or the Lass of Richmond Hill? Far from it. Traditional to him meant traditional jazz, free from further inventions and additions to this variable mode of attack upon the ears and the emotions. He was no deviationist in din.

But is skiffle so rapidly disappearing? My latest information from this musical front is that 'rock-and-rollers' and skifflers have been condensed into rifflers. The Riffle Band, of which I have this news, uses an oil-can as well as a wash-board among its instrumental equipment. The personal appearance of rifflers and skifflers appears, from their photographs, to demand either tousled or crew-cut hair 'styling', for young men have 'hair styles' nowadays, not haircuts. Also essential are hill-billy shirts of a vaguely tartanish look, the weave, as Highlanders would say, of Clan McSkiffle. But there are no bagpipes yet.

SMEAR

No politician or public figure is now described as 'unfairly attacked'. He is 'smeared' or the victim of a 'smear' campaign. This is one of the words that has radically changed its meaning. It was originally applied to anointing with oil and was a spiritually cleansing process: later the doctors took smear over from the clerics and smeared a wound to clean it and avert infection. Later still, the word 'became mud', as we say. Our unpleasant minds could only think of a smear as something ugly or dirty. So came the profanation of a word once signifying purity and the healing of spirit and flesh.

There comes a time in the history of many words when their wrongful employment has gone on so long that the dictionary has to accept that usage as established. Officious, for example, began its life as an adjective for the zealous and dutiful person: but since observance of duty is frequently and tiresomely over-worked, officious was applied to those moved by their excessive zeal to be fussy and interfering nuisances. So the old meaning has been entirely discarded, and an epithet of admiration turned into one of censure. In the same way smear has lost its healthiness and sanctity and has been dipped and fouled in the mud of malice.

SOPHISTICATED

As a student of fashion, its journalese and its idiom I am always encountering Sophistication. I have just seen a reference to 'these cocktail shoes with sophisticated heels'. Why cocktails can better, or only, be absorbed on a foundation of special footwear, it is difficult to see. But of sophistication there is much to be noted, since the word has now completely betrayed its own exalted origin. Heels, thus described, ought not to be slender, lofty, gay and giddy, but flat, sober, solid and scholarly. Instead of being the companions of 'the social glass' and of frivolous chatter, they better befit the cell of the recluse than the salon of the convivial.

The Greek word for Wisdom was Sophia. (Hence our girls called Sophia should be scholars all.) From Sophia came the Sophist. He was a man who taught wisdom as a profession. But the teaching of wisdom by the ancient Greek Sophists, serious and honest at first, became associated with instruction in mental cunning, in quibbling, and in the craft of making the worse case seem the better. The Sophists, teaching or misleading all who would pay them for a course of mental training, won a bad name as corrupters of young minds. Thus sophist, sophistry and sophistical have been turned into terms for intellectual chicanery and then used for general disparagement.

The idea of something 'phoney' had dominated the use of these words in English by Shakespeare's time. To Sir Francis Bacon 'sophistry and affectation' were linked together as the vices of shallow University wits. In the eighteenth century 'to sophisticate' had gone even further to the bad. It was employed to signify adulteration of goods as well as debasing of moral and logical standards. In this sense sophisticated gin was 'hooch'.

Accordingly, in our own time, it has come about that 'a sophisticated girl', instead of being wisdom's child, is not an 'egg-head'. She is more notable for flighty conduct than for serious contemplation. I have heard it said of a young lady that she was sophisticated with the implication that 'she may be wooed, she may be won', without consideration of matrimony, or even that she was ready to do such wooing on her own initiative. She is what Shakespeare called 'a daughter of the game': the same critic of the sex further observed, through the mouth of Hamlet, who often seems to speak

Shakespeare's mind when he speaks his own, that the young ladies of this kind are notable for a giddy kind of gait and speech:

> You jig, you amble and you lisp.

He may have had in mind that 'altitude of a chopine', which Hamlet comments upon in his talk with the players. Chopines were built-up shoes used by the players to give extra height. So there were play-boy heels, if not cocktail heels, in his period.

During the centuries Sophistication has slipped down from the clever brain to the wayward heart and thence to the party-going feminine foot. The sophisticated heels of modern modishness are those on which the fair go teetering to their gaieties. Stiletto heels they are sometimes called, which sounds more painful than hedonistic. We have thus toddled, cocktail-bent, quite a distance from the original and austere Sophia.

SPIFFLICATE

'PROBABLY fanciful', says the *Oxford English Dictionary*. I suppose that one would call it schoolboy English and a little out of date at that. Spifflicate is defined as crush or destroy, but its significance is not necessarily lethal, or even violent. The meaning may be no more than 'get the better of'. One could surely spifflicate an opponent at any game, including spillikins, that peaceful pastime of our grandparents, played with slender chips or spills that have to be unravelled singly from their tangle without moving the mass. It was not a suitable sport for the impatient or for those whose hands had become unsteady owing to senility, alcohol, or nervous tension. In this age of cerebrotony do people still have time and a steady finger for spillikins? It is a game maladjusted, if we must use that word, to the era of supersonic speeds in the air and of their attendant noises and vibrations. Or does the jet-pilot, when relaxing, find spillikins an abiding comfort?

Returning to spifflicate I note that *Oxford's* idea of the word as

fancy's child is challenged. 'A philologist of many years' standing'
— don't philologists ever sit to practise their delightful profession
or hobby? — joined in a recent discussion about spifflication in the
correspondence columns of the *Sunday Times*. He gave the word
a medieval origin, claiming that spiffing was a common ploy of the
thirteenth and fourteenth centuries. Spiffing, said the philologist,
Mr Marshall of Lincoln, is a corruption of spy-fowling. The great
milords were above spiffing, but 'the lesser members of noble
households, with specially made light longbows, would shoot on
the wing the "spy-fowl" or "prycock"'. The rolls of manor houses,
it seems, mentioned this sport as common among 'the lower strata'.
To spiff with an arrow a bird in flight must have needed a hand as
steady as that required for the sedentary and domestic recreation of
spillikins. There appears to be a likely derivation here.

Not long ago there was another kind of spiffing. Spiffy, as an
adjective for smart and elegant, is dated by *Oxford* at 1860 and long
after that spiffing was slang for anything first-rate. To the young a
new bike was spiffing, but these terms of approbation do not last
long. Spiffing has vanished and the esteemed bike, promoted to be
a motor bike of formidable speed, then became top-hole, wizard,
or whizzo.

For spifflication, in the sense of outwitting or overcoming, I now
see rumbling. When the famous West Indian cricketer and much-
feared spin-bowler, Ramadhin, failed to oust the English batsmen,
May and Cowdrey, from a record partnership in a Test Match, I
saw a headline proudly announcing: 'Ramadhin Rumbled.' To
rumble is to discover, detect, fathom. The secret of the hazardous
spin was out and certainly May and Cowdrey did achieve, on that
occasion at Edgbaston, a considerable feat not only of rumbling but
of spifflication.

STENTORIAN

My note on ovate and ovation might have included the adjective
stentorian. A speaker who has addressed the public in stentorian

tones may receive stentorian cheers. This adjective is one of the many relics of the classical tradition in our education. Its survival is the more curious since Stentor was a quite unimportant character in the ancient Greek epic poems about the war against Troy for the recapture of Helen, the stolen or errant wife of Menelaus, King of Sparta. The major characters of Homer's tale have not bestowed abiding epithets on their particular qualities. We do not talk of Odyssean cunning, Achillean sulks, or even of Helenic beauty. The Trojan hero, Hector, has begotten no word Hectorian. His name in Greek meant the defender or the man who holds fast. It is difficult to see any proper connection between this brave, ill-fated warrior and our verb hector which means to bluster, bully and domineer.

But two small characters in the two great Epics, *Iliad* and *Odyssey*, have emerged and lived on, thus doing what the great figures failed to do. One is Proteus, the Old Man of the Sea, who makes a brief appearance in the *Odyssey*. Since he could alter his shape and looks instantaneously in order to serve his need, the adjective protean is still applied to quick-change artists on the stage and to other practitioners of rapid veering with all the winds of fortune and compulsions of necessity or advantage. We know of protean politicians.

Stentor, in the *Iliad*, was no mighty general like Agamemnon or beef-witted lord like Ajax. He was the herald, the man who did the public speaking, the issuer of challenges. He was the military version of our old town criers. His voice was reputed to be fifty times as loud as that of any other man in the Grecian host. In our times of microphones and broadcasting a quiet voice will do for the most important of public statements. A whisper can go round the world. Then Stentor was very useful as the Big Noise of his side and his din has come roaring down the centuries. Tones are still stentorian.

Stentor was 'an epic figure', as we say, in the true sense of that phrase. His lungs were resonant in an epic poem. The Greek word epos meant a word: hence our eponymous, an adjective for a word or name which gave its name to another thing. Hamlet, for example, is the eponymous hero of the play of *Hamlet*. But epos, having signified one word, went on to be the title of an enormous number of words. So the epos was used to designate a long, wordy, narrative poem which we still call an epic. Because such poems usually dealt with the mighty deeds of the legendary heroes we have converted the adjective epic into a synonym for anything outstanding, anything that is 'big news'. Newspaper men have been especially faithful to epic because it is short and fits easily into headlines.

So film-stars, when mobbed by their devotees, are the source of 'epic scenes'. Footballers score epic goals and cricketers make epic centuries. These, in their turn, evoke stentorian cheers. What long-continued tribute do we pay, mostly without knowing it, to the myths, chronicles and characters of the ancient Greeks.

SUBTOPIAN AND UTOPIAN

THE untidy word, Subtopian, is continually turning up in articles about town planning, urban squalor and so forth. It is a new-comer and its manufacturer should have known better than to mix the Latin sub, meaning under, with the Greek topos, meaning place, and out of that mixed marriage to produce an unrecognizable child.

As Subtopian is too young to be in the dictionaries I had to ask an artist to tell me what it meant. He said that it was short for sub-Utopian. Assuming that our new towns and housing estates are meant to be Utopian, i.e. ideal, the kind of planning and building which misses that high level but is not too bad could be Subtopian. The adjective in this case confers moderate praise.

But others plainly do not agree with this definition, for I frequently see Subtopian applied to the architectural underworld, the nasty mess, the town at its most squalid. Here the adjective is one of angry dismissal. Because of this uncertainty about meaning, I would never use this new invention.

Utopia is our version of the Greek for Nowhere and has been

the title given to the ideal communities imagined by philosophers ever since the time of Sir Thomas More (1478-1535), an early English visionary in that line of country. H. G. Wells poured out Utopias too, but nowadays we dare not look forward to heaven on earth. We find glimpses of hell in our midst, such as Orwell's *1984*, to be more plausible. In Orwell's book people are living not in subtopian but in sub-human conditions.

Perhaps we may cheer up before long and go back to buying cheerful Utopias for reading and discussion in our homes, which I shall not call Subtopian.

SUNDRIES

I AM always fascinated by the mention of Sundries in a balance sheet. If I put it to my Income Tax Authority that at the end of my claim for professional expenses I proposed to insert a further item of £150 for Sundries, he would not, I fancy, be sympathetic. Yet chartered accountants seem lightly to tolerate an entry thus labelled in the disbursals of the Society for the protection or promotion of this and that. Sundries, £247 10s. It seems an easy way of keeping the books. So, when I check my own expenditure in a vague, amateurish way and notice, as I always do, that there is less in the wallet than I fancied, I murmur, 'Ah, Sundries again'.

Sundry is an ancient and august word. 'The Scripture moveth us in sundry places to acknowledge and confess our manifold sins and wickedness.' Sundry things were things sundered, put apart and so, in the course of time, miscellaneous. There is always an obvious need for some loosely inclusive term for a number of minor matters, and we have a fair supply of them. Miscellaneous and miscellany proclaim their own gathering of 'all and sundry', of 'bits and pieces'. Paraphernalia is a queer child of the ancient Greek bedroom. It originally meant the bits beside the Hellenic bed, 'para' meaning alongside and 'pherne' couch. So the paraphernalian possessions were the things in the bedroom, dresses, ornaments, powder

H

and paste, that is to say the property allowed by law to a wife when married women were denied most legal rights of ownership.

Later on paraphernalia came to be a term for dresses and trappings; they might be the companions of considerable pomp and ceremony. But a contemptuous note has crept into the usage of the word. A husband asking his wife, 'What's all this paraphernalia?' would nowadays imply a lot of petty articles which were more of a nuisance than a glory. We have long ago forgotten about the legal origin of the term: paraphernalian articles are now the raw material of a clutter.

For a medley of things there is another phrase, half Latin instead of Greek. That is 'omnium gatherum', which is a playful telescoping of the Latin omnium, meaning 'of all', and the English gathering. Picturesque among the Sundry synonyms is the Scottish clamjamphrie. That was first a lordly description of a rabble of inferior persons. Next it was a gabble of worthless chatter. The crushing together of clamping and jamming in this word suggests a heated gaggle and cackle of human geese at the most tedious kind of cocktail party. Last it was applied to a mass of small articles, trumpery stuff. Jamieson's *Scottish Dictionary* quotes: 'Did ye stop till the end of the roup [auction]?' 'Ay, a' was selled but the clamjamphrie.'

The Anglo-French gallimaufry is in the same class. First it was a hodge-podge of assorted food: it came to include any hodge-podge of persons or possessions. If we are now to use 'paraphernalia' accurately and according to its Greek origin (i.e. to convey 'bed-alongside-things'), the ancient commode and that favourite modern commodity, the Bedside Book, would be among its just recipients.

SUNFOLK

THERE is gallantry, as well as simplicity, in the title Sunfolk when used in Great Britain. (I write this at the end of a murky winter following a summer dismally short of sunshine.) The Sunfolk of

whom I have been reading, do not, I am glad to notice, call themselves Heliophilists or practitioners of Heliology. If in America a
strip-tease artist can be known as an ecdysiast (Greek, ekduein —
to put off), it is likely that the Sunfolk of the Golden West will be
no less classical and will be labelled with some form of helio-
centricity. But in most of America the addicts of exposure can justify
their pastime since they have a considerable source of radiation-
supply, as they probably call our modest sunbeam. To practise
Nudism in our 'misty-moisty' island seems, even more than the
widower's remarriage, to be a triumph of hope over experience.

To return to our Sunfolk. In the East Midlands a society with
this title keeps a field for its nudist camp. Annoyed at the rates
levied on their Garden of Eden, the members applied for relief and
won their case. It was decided that they owned 'a playing-field'
within the meaning of the Rating and Valuation Act. Herein there
seems to be a hint to others who regard their landed property as
overburdened. Let them be Playful Sunfolk. To be 'de-bagged' is
to be de-rated.

TAXONOMY

AMERICAN books send me to my dictionary more often than do
English ones. That is not because they use American slang, which
is usually vivid and pictorial, but because they will use classical or
bogus-classical terms which are simply a nuisance. Here is a typical
example. In a book I have just read, which discussed coloured
people and the problems of racialism, an authority on slavery in
American history began a paragraph thus: 'By 1738 biology had
chimed in. Linnaeus, father of taxonomy ... '

I suppose that I should have been able immediately to define
taxonomy, which is 'that department of science, or of a particular
science or subject which consists in, or relates to, classification'.
Linnaeus, then, was early in this business of making lists and clas-
sifying. Why not say so? The work quoted had enormous sales in

the U.S.A. What percentage of its readers could have defined taxonomy without a dip into the dictionary?

Doubtless many thought that it had something to do with taxes. But our word tax is simply a variant for task, and what a burden that sort of task can be we know better than any previous generation of mankind. Tax next came to mean another species of burden, a price-list or tariff: hence the taximeter which measures that kind of load and has given us the taxi-cab now so internationally known as the taxi.

But taxonomy has nothing to do with tasks, loads or vehicles. It comes from the Greek taxis which had a number of diverse meanings, such as a manipulative surgical operation, a company of soldiers, and, more generally, an arrangement or setting in order. From the last comes the taxonomy which lays down the nomos or law about drawing up lists and so is the science of classification. Perhaps I should be grateful to the author of the book which I have just mentioned; by sending me to the lexicon he has given me a deal of side-line information. When I next take a cab to visit a manipulative surgeon, I may be vague as to my physical trouble but I shall know what we are both talking about when I cry 'taxi' and he remarks that it is a case for immediate taxis.

TOGGLE

THE toggle has come ashore with the duffel-coat. Duffel is a strong cloth with a thick nap and, like so many cloths and garments, it long ago took its name from the place of its early weaving, in this case a town near Antwerp. Toggle also has a Low Country sound and one might guess it to have come from the Dutch. But it is really a native and it is explained as a form of taggle and tangle. In function it was, aboard ship and in harbour, a short pin passing through the loop or eye of a rope or the aperture of a bolt. Now it loops the front of a popular form of overcoat.

Usage has been unkind to tags and taggles. Shakespeare called the rabble the tag-rag people and there is an old song which tells of the raggle-taggle gipsies. But taggles are no longer a sign of raggedness or squalor; as toggles they have come up in the world while leaving the sea. Now they are quite a fashionable adjunct to the winter covering of land-animals and their hearts of oak.

Tangle, though it may at times represent an ugly mess, has always had a certain wild beauty inherent in its complications. John Milton was surely not showing discourtesy to Neaera when he wrote of sporting with the tangles of her hair. The author of the very popular words for an old Scottish air was giving his praise to the Hebrides when he wrote of 'the tangle of the isles'. But few would care to sport with the toggles on a fair lady's scalp or think the West of Scotland duly honoured by a reference to the toggle of its islands.

TOXIC

'I'm so toxic,' said a feminine character in a wisecracking type of play, 'that the flowers wither when I go into the garden.' The poor creature must indeed have been in a bad way; but we are lucky if we have never felt toxic in our own persons and afflicted with that leaden feeling of apathy and drowsiness which some poison in the system can create.

Toxicology, from the Greek toxon, is the science of poisons and even people who know some Greek may reasonably wonder whether toxicology and toxophily are not both concerned with this more baleful kind of chemistry. But a toxophilist is no devotee of subtle murder, an arsenic-and-old-lace type who buys weed-killer for his wealthy aunt; nor is he a suicidal specimen with an impulse to swallow sleeping-tablets by the hundred. We must think rather of the archers, once the bowmen of ancient Greece and medieval Agincourt and now the pacific sportsmen and sportswomen of long green lawns and gaily coloured targets, the folk who fleet the time, and their arrows, carefully.

Yet toxicology and toxophily are cousins. The Greek word toxon meant a bow. Because barbaric peoples smeared their arrows with poison, the weapon which fired these missiles was turned into the source and then the symbol of poisons. The word's origin in archery was forgotten, and the dealer in toxic affairs was seen as a poisoner, while the toxophilists of our time remained innocent amateurs of the well-directed arrow. None should be less toxic than they are, since sureness of eye and steadiness of hand are their necessities.

Intoxication, therefore, meant poisoning in deadly earnest before it became associated with a less lethal and more pleasing form of absorption. Whether or not we think alcohol to be poison, the word shares with toxon a much less guilty start in life.

Alcohol began as an Arabic word for a powder used by women to stain the eyelids for beauty's sake. Then, 'by extension', it was oddly employed to signify an essence or spirit, especially the pure spirit of distilled liquors. And so, just as we move from archery to one kind of poison, we are carried, by verbal accident, from make-up to inebriation.

In the vocabulary of toxication and its remedies there occurs the old word Mithridate, which meant an antidote against poison. Mithridates was King of Pontus in Asia Minor (120-63 B.C.). He gave the Romans a lot of trouble and was infamous for his cruelties and massacres. One might think, therefore, that a Mithridate was a name for some drug intensely toxic: as a matter of fact, it was just the reverse. The ruthless Mithridates was himself terrified of being poisoned and believed that he could obtain immunity by taking small and gradually increasing doses of poison, as we seek immunity for sundry diseases by inoculation with a small dose of them. So a Mithridate became the label for a miniature toxon expected to defeat any major toxication. Its object was to cure, not kill.

TRANQUILLIZER

I⊤ is said that the consumption of tranquillizers has become general in the United States of America, whose business men, when most busy, must, like Othello, cry: 'Farewell, the tranquil mind.' The effort to recapture calm is made with pocketable pills; even more than Woman, these serve as ministering angels 'when pain and sorrow wring the brow'.

Tranquillizers, I am told, rapidly and effectively convey the 'don't-care-a-damn' feeling so necessary to harassed 'executives'. They derive, not only from the chemist's art, but also from an apt and beautiful adjective. We are lucky in our epithets of easement. Tranquil and serene come softly breathing to the ear. Tennyson's 'Passionless bride, divine tranquillity' soothes by its very sound. Chapman's translation of Homer gave Keats a 'pure serene', which is a musical emollient of unhappy stress, but I do not expect the gulpers of a tranquillizer to try poetry as a remedy for their tension.

The termination '-izer' is harsh and a disturber of the peace. I hope that we shall never insult the exquisite word serene by asking for a serenizer at the drug-store. It is remarkable that a fair word can be so quickly fouled. Serenade adds to the charm of serene: serenizer does not diminish charm: it destroys it. Tranquil has its own beatitude in its own two syllables: add two more and the tranquillizer has lost its balm. But it is hard to think of another name for the kindly capsule that will knit up 'the ravelled sleave of care'. The Shakespearian sleave, by the way, is a filament of silk and has nothing to do with the sleeve of Macbeth's night-shirt.

The Greek coma is one of the serene and tranquil words which we have spoilt by applying it to an inert and senseless condition. The *Oxford English Dictionary* calls coma a pathological term and defines it as 'a state of unnatural, heavy, prolonged sleep with complete unconsciousness and a slow, stertorous breathing, frequently ending in death'. Here is tranquillity 'in over-plus', an ugly matter to eye and ear. Yet coma is as gracious a word as tranquil or serene. To the Greeks it suggested no pathological swoon, with grunts and snoring added. Sappho used it of a pure and pastoral repose, and the words 'coma catarrei' (I must give the sound of the phrase in English lettering since few would now recognize it in the Greek) make lullaby music, as sweetly hypnotic as the scene she described. This fragment of her verse I have translated.

> Cool is the stream: the apple trees
> Rustle and quiver in the breeze.
> Down from the branches gently creep
> The trance of calm and boon of sleep.

Relaxed in her Lesbian orchard Sappho did not need a tranquillizer. Helen of Troy did require, and, according to Homer, did take, something of that kind, when back in Sparta, reconciled to her naturally resentful husband, Menelaus, and yet vexed with old memories and anguishes. She had found, during her wanderings in the homeward return from burned and ruined Troy, an Egyptian salve which, dropped in the wine, would wipe out such distress. Was it an opiate? Down the centuries recourse to the tranquillizing poppy has been common among restless and brain-sickly folk and often with beneficial results, if not to the taker, at least to posterity, since laudanum has been an aid to some of the best of our prose and poetry. Sappho did not mention such medicaments. But she may have known of both opium and hemp, since those were familiar tranquillizers in the Homeric Age, six hundred years before her time. However, in the green shade, the plashing stream and the wind from the Aegean Sea sufficed on summer afternoons. Coma ensued — and gracefully. For grace is the prevailing word in what is left of Sappho's poetry. One does not imagine heavy breathing or hear the gross echo of a snore impinge upon the Lesbian peace.

The Greeks did not live in a period of bustle and hustle: one does not think of them as victims of neurosis. But tranquillity was an ideal that haunted them. They had their glimpses of lotus-eating felicity: this diet, according to Homer, abolished nostalgia. The consumers of the honeyed fruit of the plant only wish to stay where they were, browsing and drowsing, all passion spent, all quest of glory and adventure laid aside. The cry of the Tennysonian lotus-eaters was 'Let us alone ... We will not wander more'. This drowsy diet would appeal to those nervous victims of the day's work and the morrow's cares who run to the modern chemist for his calming capsules. The tranquillizer is nothing new: in Sparta and in Lotos-land the Greeks had a word for it.

TRICHOLOGICAL

WHILE in a car I noticed in front of me a van on whose back door was written in capital letters:

CORRECTLY TRICHOLOGICAL

HAIR PRODUCTS

What, I naturally wondered, were its contents?

Trichology, a word from the Greek, means 'the study of the structure, functions and diseases of the hair'. So a trichological product might be a student with a diploma in the craft of hair-care or the kind of books and lectures contributing to that learning. But I fancied that in this case trichological was just a pompous poly-syllable meaning hairy. Then the question arose whether a hair product, correctly or incorrectly trichological, meant something made with hair for the head, i.e. a toupee or wig, or something made with hair for other purposes. Was the van carrying pillows and mattresses? Another product of hair is dandruff, but that would hardly be carried off in vans nor could it be 'trichologically correct'. Again, hair products might be products for the hair, such as lotions and scalp-fertilizers. This last seemed the most probable solution.

The van had been labelled in the idiom of newspaper headline English which cuts out prepositions for brevity's sake and thereby creates some puzzling results in what is really a special department of 'telegraphese'. In his excellent pamphlet on 'Newspaper English', Sir Linton Andrews, the editor of the *Yorkshire Post*, has collected some notable examples of this compression. One is 'Gang War: Spot Judge'. This turned out to mean that the judge in the trial of a gentleman known as Jack Spot had made some remarks on the gangs at war with each other in and around Soho. Another enigma cited was '£20 Union Carpets Protest Pinner'. This had nothing to do with a small trade union whose funds ran only to £20 or with a union whose annual subscription was of that amount. Nor had any protest been made about carpets at the town of Pinner. The correct interpretation was that Mr Pinner, a member of a union which had given £20 to a fund for the succour of Cypriots, had protested against this grant and been disciplined or carpeted by the union for his temerity in objecting to the gift. 'Trichologically correct hair products' seem to be in this class of mystification.

WACKY

I come across the word Wacky nowadays, in the writings of those who find their raw (or refined) material in 'Nite-Spots'. My chief authority on these matters is Mr Rex North of the *Sunday Pictorial*, who gives me a deal of useful and lively information about who is who and what is wackily what.

Wacky, I gather from studying its various uses, means crazy, but crazy in a smart expensive way. Expensive parties can be wacky: I do not think that a beano of down-and-outs could be so described. In an American play called *A Hatful of Rain* a dope-crazy lady who charged about with nothing under her (fortunately ample) mink was called a Wacky Blonde. She satisfied both needs of the adjective, being wealthy as well as wild.

It is natural that smart writers describing smart people should want some new adjectives, since fashion must move on and words for the gay and costly soon get stale. In recent years I have seen this kind of elegance in persons or places described as Ritzy or Very Mink; but Ritzy is 'out'. Previous terms of this kind were either worked to death, e.g. swell, or drifted down to the school-room level, e.g. nob and nobby, posh and swish.

Posh was first of all slang for money, and this came to signify what money, or extravagance, could buy. Swish does suggest the rustle of fine silks — as well as the sound of a cane. In J. B. Priestley's books and plays Yorkshire folk, when being contemptuous of Southerners, dismiss their way of life as 'all la-di-da', a word which became popular after its use in a Victorian music-hall song.

A much earlier word of this kind was alamode. That went down-hill socially when it was much used by caterers to describe a cheap and popular dish called 'Beef alamode', 'bits of beef boiled down into a stew' and so not at all wacky or Ritzy.

The war-time and R.A.F. use of Wacko for excellent presumably created the better, less crazy meaning of wacky. The only word in the English dictionary at all close to wacky is wacke, which is a kind of rock and not likely to be connected with social grandeur. Shakespeare was rude about fashion-mongers, but he did not have any inclusive adjective for them. He thought of them in terms of an insect; to him the fops were water-flies. Presumably he had the glittering dragon-fly in mind, wackiest of insects.

Other words in favour with journalists writing about wacky goings-on are lush and plushy. Film-stars are interviewed in lush hotels. Lush can fairly be used of expensive suites and their fur-nishings. Its older form was lash, which meant slack, loose, or soft: in its altered form of lush it was applied to rich growths and luxur-iant vegetation. Then the greenery was forgotten and the luxury remembered. Lash, as a verb, meant not only to whip but to squander. Hence our lashings of cream or of money, constituents of lush feeding and lush living.

Plush was a term for cloth with plentiful nap on it. Is plush upholstery now the distinguishing feature of really wacky apart-ments? Yet the word, because of its similarity to lush, is often employed, especially in its adjectival form, plushy, to signify

lashings of lushness in the Ritzy apartments, in which the interviewers find the wacky fair ones, 'dripping in mink'.

WET AND WAFFLE

WHEN I was at Oxford there was a habit of describing men without
much apparent personality as dim, and I remember being told by
Lord Keynes that this word was also much used with that meaning
at Cambridge. It was a considerable assumption on the speaker's
part to regard himself as radiantly bright. Of course a supposedly
dim character may well be Thomas Gray's 'gem of purest ray
serene', which 'the dark, unfathomed caves of ocean bear', and may
thus be doomed, by lack of exhibitionism, to blush unseen. In life
the showmanship may often be all, or very nearly, all. That is a
pity, but is also, I fear, true.

The new mode is to call the supposedly dim person wet or even,
with greater disparagement, a drip. Is it implied by the dismissal
of an acquaintance as damp that he has a nervous habit of breaking
out in perspiration? Some of the over modest and over apprehensive
may be thus bedewed on social or challenging occasions and so
manifest their fears in their faces, but I should have thought that
the wet one, or drip, was pictured chiefly as pallid and flabby, like
an over-boiled potato. Somebody long ago established the same
idea in talking of a wet blanket, but it refers rather to a depressing
action than to a dreary person.

The wet figure, when he rises to his feet in public life, is well
described as waffling. To waffle, as I understand it, is to speak with
a vague benevolence but to no purpose. The waffler is not misleading his audience for some crafty end; he is only muddled and
muddling. Chairmen, who from a sense of public duty conscien-
tiously preside over meetings whose business they do not fully
understand, have to be cautious and so are inevitably driven to some
initial waffling when they open the proceedings, and may do so
again on concluding the session. But that does not prove them to

be in all things wet. They have merely been too kind in accepting the taxing business of presiding over gatherings. Some of the subsequent speakers may, with less excuse, be total drips or even cascades of drippery, waffling on to the embarrassment of the chairman and the tedium of the company.

The same idea of watery ineffectiveness underlay the old use of soppy. There was a time, which according to the dictionary began at the turn of the century, when young women talked of dim young men as soppy, but I fancy that the word has now vanished from our slang. Soppy also implied sentimentality. A too lush or romantic story could be dismissed as soppy, and a declaration of affection might be met with the request, 'Oh, don't be so soppy', if the fair one had someone less moist in view. But she would not have said moist. One adjective of an aquatic nature never used, as far as I know, in adverse description of a character has been this one. Did anyone ever speak of a moist young man? It occurs to me that one of the most unpleasant forms of wetness is a thaw, but I have never heard a dim and damp person described as a thaw.

Gilbert's 'greenery-yallery, Grosvenor Gallery, foot-in-the-grave young man' was, perhaps, what we would call an arty drip. And he could doubtless have waffled at length about modern painting. Curiously, to call a person desiccated, i.e. lacking in sap, is to make a suggestion similar to that implied in calling him wet. But the wetness of a waffling drip is not sap. It is flat and tepid water.

ZIP

ZIP was a raccoon in the world of Uncle Remus and also the name of a song and dance favoured by American popular minstrels. The famous American 'Turkey in the sand' has a tune borrowed from an earlier song called 'Zip-Coon'. Zipping is such an expressive word for speed that its common usage was inevitable, both as verb and noun. An inventor in the early nineteen-twenties used the term for his rapidly adjusted and rapidly popular fastenings. We are always zipping-up something nowadays and the manufacturers of buttons, strings, straps and laces for body-wear and footwear, as well as for bag and baggage, must have cursed the incursion of the zip.

ZOMBIE and ZOOT

'A PERSON lacking will or imagination, usually of very low intelligence.' Zombie is an ugly and a sinister word and its nastiness separates it from the comparatively innocent circus in whose arena the twerps, drips and clots exhibit their follies. The original zombie was a Central African snake-deity who could re-animate the dead. Next he was the revived corpse and spook as well. This ghost, transported to West Indian superstition, was of a formidable kind, retaining some human solidity and resembling disinterred remains on the prowl.

Still, he has had his fanciers. The Elizabethan stage was a zombies' barrack-square, since its regiment of spectres came on parade in such corporeal form. In productions of *Macbeth* Banquo's ghost is usually and rightly presented as a pallid piece of decomposing body. The 'dead corse', revisiting the glimpses of the moon, making night hideous, and stirring 'thoughts beyond the reaches of our souls', was a constant pleasure of the old playgoers: but the spectral members of this Ancient Order of Grave-breakers and Sepulchral Escapists were not fools. Hamlet's father stalked the battlements of Elsinore with a zombie's aspect, but he was certainly not a lout or an idiot. It is the combined suggestion of the deathly and the doltish that makes the idea of a zombie so odious to those of us who know what the word means. Fortunately the source of the name has been largely forgotten and when we now talk or hear of a zombie we think only of a sub-human and lumpish creature, and do not consider him in relation to his tomb or his ghost.

Players of the spelling-game called Scrabble are always glad to plant a word containing the letter Z on the board and gladder still to add further letters to a word with Z in it, since these manœuvres are very profitable in the reckoning of points. Hence, should someone have put down Zoo, chances to add to it are eagerly sought. Aeroplanes go zooming up to the benefit of a player holding the letter M. Then there is Zoot for those with a T to spare. It sounds ghastly, and Zombies, who began by being ghostly, and became ghastly, may be the wearers thereof.

A Zoot Suit is defined as 'one of extreme cut'. The trousers reach up to the armpits and descend to be wide at the knees and narrow at the ankles. The coat is a knee-length one, with padded shoulders, billowing sleeves and diagonally cut pockets. Certain kinds of performer who ululate, perspire and weep in front of microphones have been zoot suit addicts. I should put them in the zombie class, but before this appears in print there is a fair chance that Zoots will be 'oot', as a Scot would say.

My latest sartorial adjective is snazzy. I have just read of an actor assuming a snazzy jacket when playing the part of a superior species of Teddy Boy. Teddy Boys were oafs named after the Edwardian tailoring which they revived in exaggerated form. Like Zoots, they may be only short-lived and well forgotten in a month or two after this was written. Meanwhile, what snazzy means I can only guess. And at the vision my eyes dazzle.